بسم الله الرحمن الرحيم

The BURDA

The BURDA

IMAM SHARAF AD-DIN
AL-BUSIRI

with

THE MUDARIYYA

THE MUHAMMADIYYA

Translated by Aziza Spiker

First Printed 2012
Reprinted 2013

THE BURDA
Translated by Aziza Spiker

Guidance Media
info@guidancemedia.com

Design by Guidance Media

Cover design by Quemedia
Cover picture from a page of an Ottoman handwritten manuscript of the Burda

ISBN 978-0-9550891-5-2

CONTENTS

Introduction ix

The Burda

1. On Words of Love and the Intense Suffering of Passion 3
2. A Caution about the Whims of the Self 8
3. On the Praise of the Prophet ﷺ 14
4. On his Birth ﷺ 25
5. On the Miracles that came at his Hand ﷺ 30
6. On the Nobility of the Qur'an and its Praise 36
7. On the Prophet's Night Journey and Ascension ﷺ 42
8. On the Martial Struggle of the Prophet ﷺ 47
9. On Seeking Intercession through the Prophet ﷺ 55
10. On Intimate conversation and cherished hopes 60

The Mudariyya 67

The Muhammadiyya 85

INTRODUCTION

Imam Sharaf ad-Dīn al-Būṣīrī, born in Egypt in 696/1212, and of Moroccan Berber origin, was a poet whose poems in praise of the Prophet Muḥammad ﷺ are still sung today throughout the Muslim world. For those who know them, they need little introduction, as their beauty is revealed in the gatherings where they are sung.

This small handbook has been produced with the Arabic text, transliteration and English translation, designed to facilitate participation and understanding for those not familiar with the Arabic language. While it is certainly true that attending the gatherings where Būṣīrī's poems are sung is a great blessing in itself, to be able to actually take part in the singing and with understanding of his words is an even greater blessing.

Imam Būṣīrī's best known works are the *Burda*, the *Muḍariyya*, the *Muḥammadiyya* and the *Ḥamziyya*, the first three of which are included in the present volume.

The *Burda*, known in English as the 'Poem of the Cloak', is also called 'Celestial Lights in Praise of the Best of Creation'. It is his most famous work, and was so named following a dream which Imam Būṣīrī had after he was partially paralysed by a stroke. Following this change of fortune, he had written the *Burda*, longing for greater nearness to the Prophet ﷺ and in regret that some of his former life had been spent as a court poet, where he felt he had wasted his time in the flattery of worldly figures. He would sing the *Burda* over and over again, and on one occasion, falling asleep, he was granted a dream which was to transform his life.

In his dream, Būṣīrī saw the Prophet ﷺ who cast his cloak over him. When he awoke, he found himself completely cured. To add to this miraculous occurrence, when he ventured outside, he met a dervish on the road, who asked him for the poem, recited part of it and revealed that he knew of its existence through having heard it in a vision, recited before the Prophet himself.

The *Burda* itself consists of ten chapters, the first of which expresses Būṣīrī's own passionate love for the Prophet ﷺ and the second, his feelings of unworthiness, regret for past errors, and advice on handling the ego or *nafs*, which is always calling its owner to evil. The central portions of the poem are similar in theme to the traditional *mawlid* poems, which are sung in the month of *Rabiᶜa'l-Awwal* in celebration of the Prophet's birth ﷺ with different sections on the Prophet's virtues; his birth; his miracles; the noble Qur'an which he received as revelation; his night journey and his martial struggle. The last two sections are Būṣīrī's plea for the Prophet's intercession on the Last Day, despite his many wrong actions, and finally an appeal, first to the Prophet for protection, and then to God's mercy as the ultimate hope of salvation.

Following the main text of the *Burda* are seven verses added at a later date, which are traditionally sung in some parts of the Muslim world, asking that God's good pleasure and forgiveness be granted to the four rightly-guided caliphs; the Prophet's Family; his Companions; the 'Followers' (the generation that followed the Companions) and all of the Muslims. Praise of God is then followed by a final supplication that all of our difficulties be eased by the one hundred and sixty verses of the *Burda* through God's boundless Generosity.

The *Muḍariyya* is a shorter poem, asking God to bestow blessings upon the Prophet Muḥammad and all the other Prophets and Messengers, upon his Family, his Companions and all the Muslims. He asks for the multiplication of these blessings by the many different types of animate and inanimate created things in the heavens and the earth. He then recollects his own state of wrongdoing, and begs for forgiveness for himself, for the Muslims, and for all their parents, families and neighbours, adding, 'For all of us, O my Master, are in great need of forgiveness.'

The *Muḥammadiyya* is the shortest of the three works, and is a beautiful expression of the Prophet's noble qualities ﷺ in which every line begins with the name Muḥammad. The poem itself is a proof of one of its verses, which tells us that just to mention him 'brings refreshment to our souls.'

The words of these poems wait only for the hearts of the lovers of the Prophet to bring them alive. They describe the sublime characteristics of the one most beloved to the Lord of the Worlds, the one whom all Muslims seek to emulate, Muḥammad, peace and blessings be upon him. We are told in the Qur'an that he was sent 'as a mercy to all the worlds'[1], and that he was created with 'a magnificent nature'.[2] He is Muḥammad, the Praiseworthy; he is *Khayr al-Bariyya* – the Best of Creation.

I would like to acknowledge my gratitude to all those who have contributed their time, energy and expertise to help bring this work to fruition. May Allah bless them and reward them abundantly.

1 Qur'an - *al-Anbiya'*, 21:107

2 Qur'an - *al-Qalam*, 68:4

The Burda

CHORUS

مَولاَيَ صَلِّ وَسَلِّم دَائِماً أَبَداً
عَلَى حَبِيبِكَ خَيْرِ الْخَلْقِ كُلِّهِمِ

Mawlāya ṣalli wa sallim dā'iman abadan
ᶜAlā ḥabībika khayri'l-khalqi kullihimi

O my Lord, bless and grant peace always and forever
Upon Your beloved one, the Best of all Creation

يَا رَبِّ صَلِّ عَلَى مُحَمَّدٍ وَ عَلَى
سَادَتِنَا آلِهِ وَصَحْبِهِ الْكِرَمِ

Ya rabbi ṣalli ᶜalā Muḥammadin wa ᶜalā
Sādatinā ālihi wa ṣaḥbihi'l-kirami

O Lord, pour Your blessings upon Muḥammad and upon
Our Masters, his Family and his noble Companions

CHAPTER ONE

On Words of Love and the Intense Suffering of Passion

أَمِنْ تَذَكُّرِ جِيرَانٍ بِذِي سَلَمِ
مَزَجْتَ دَمْعاً جَرَى مِنْ مُقْلَةٍ بِدَمِ

A min tadhakkuri jīrānin bi dhī salami
Mazajta damʿan jarā min muqlatin bi dami

1. Is it the memory of neighbours in *Dhu Salam*[1]
That has left your eyes so red with tears?

أَمْ هَبَّتِ الرِّيحُ مِنْ تِلْقَاءِ كَاظِمَةٍ
وَأَوْمَضَ الْبَرْقُ فِي الظَّلْمَاءِ مِنْ إِضَمِ

Am habbati-r-rīḥu min tilqā'i Kāẓimatin
Wa awmaḍa'l-barqu fi-ẓ-ẓalmā'i min Iḍami

2. Or is it the wind blowing from the direction of *Kāẓima*[2]
And the lightning flashing in the black night from Mount *Iḍam*?[3]

1 *Dhu Salam* - a place between Makka and Madina near Qadīd
2 *Kāẓima* - the name of an area near Madina
3 Mount *Iḍam* - a mountain near Madina

فَمَا لِعَيْنَيْكَ إِنْ قُلْتَ اكْفُفَا هَمَتَا
وَمَا لِقَلْبِكَ إِنْ قُلْتَ اسْتَفِقْ يَهِمِ

Fa mā liʿaynayka in qulta kfufā hamatā
Wa mā li qalbika in qulta stafiq yahimi

3. What is the matter with your eyes, that when you tell them to refrain,
They only weep more? And your heart – when you try to rouse it,
It only becomes more bewildered

أَيَحْسَبُ الصَّبُّ أَنَّ الْحُبَّ مُنْكَتِمٌ
مَا بَيْنَ مُنْسَجِمٍ مِنْهُ وَمُضْطَرِمِ

A yaḥsabu-ṣ-ṣabbu anna'l-ḥubba munkatimun
Mā bayna munsajimin minhu wa muḍṭarimi

4. Does the one in love suppose his love can be concealed
Between pouring tears and a blazing heart?

لَوْ لَا الْهَوَى لَمْ تُرِقْ دَمْعاً عَلَى طَلَلٍ
وَلَا أَرِقْتَ لِذِكْرِ الْبَانِ وَالْعَلَمِ

Law la'l-hawa lam turiq damʿan ʿalā ṭalalin
Wa lā ariqta li dhikri'l-bāni wa'l-ʿalami

5. If not for love, your tears would not pour forth
over traces left by your beloved,
Nor would you be sleepless remembering the willow tree and the mountain

فَكَيْفَ تُنْكِرُ حُبّاً بَعْدَ مَا شَهِدَتْ
بِهِ عَلَيْكَ عُدُولُ الدَّمْعِ وَالسَّقَمِ

Fa kayfa tunkiru ḥubban ba^cda mā shahidat
Bihi ᶜalayka ᶜudūlu'd-damᶜi wa's-saqami

6. So how can you deny this love when such honest witnesses as weeping and looking gaunt have testified to it against you?

وَأَثْبَتَ الْوَجْدُ خَطَّي عَبْرَةٍ وَضَنىً
مِثْلَ الْبَهَارِ عَلَى خَدَّيْكَ وَالْعَنَمِ

Wa athbata'l-wajdu khaṭṭay ᶜabratin wa ḍanan
Mithla'l-bahāri ᶜalā khaddayka wa'l-ᶜanami

7. The agony of love has inscribed two lines of tears and grief
Upon your cheeks, pale as *bahār*[4] and red as *ᶜanam*[5]

نَعَمْ سَرَى طَيْفُ مَنْ أَهْوَى فَأَرَّقَنِي
وَالْحُبُّ يَعْتَرِضُ اللَّذَّاتِ بِالْأَلَمِ

Naᶜam sarā ṭayfu man ahwā fa arraqanī
Wa'l-ḥubbu yaᶜtariḍu'l-ladhdhāti bi'l-alami

8. Yes, a vision of the one I love came to me by night, and I could not sleep,
Oh, how love hinders the tasting of delight with its suffering!

4 Bahār - a yellow spring flower to which the complexion is likened

5 ᶜAnam - a small tree found in the Hijāz, bearing red fruits

يَا لَائِمِي فِي الْهَوَى الْعُذْرِيِّ مَعْذِرَةً
مِنِّي إِلَيْكَ وَلَوْ أَنْصَفْتَ لَمْ تَلُمِ

Yā lā'imī fi'l-hawa'l-ᶜudhriyyi maᶜdhiratan
Minnī ilayka wa law anṣafta lam talumi

9. O you who would rebuke me for this pure love, accept my excuse.
If you were truly fair, you would not reproach me at all

عَدَتْكَ حَالِيَ لَا سِرِّي بِمُسْتَتِرٍ
عَنِ الْوُشَاةِ وَلَا دَائِي بِمُنْحَسِمِ

ᶜAdatka ḥāliya lā sirrī ḅi mustatirin
ᶜAni'l-wushāti wa lā dā'ī bi munḥasimi

10. May you be spared a state such as mine! My secret cannot be concealed
From my detractors, nor will there ever be an end to my malady

مَحَّضْتَنِي النُّصْحَ لَكِنْ لَسْتُ أَسْمَعُهُ
إِنَّ الْمُحِبَّ عَنِ الْعُذَّالِ فِي صَمَمِ

Maḥḥaḍtani'n-nuṣḥa lākin lastu asmaᶜuhu
Inna'l-muḥibba ᶜani'l-ᶜudhdhāli fī ṣamami

11. You gave me sincere good counsel, but I did not hear it,
The lover is quite deaf to those who blame him

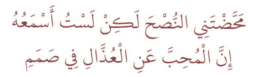

إِنِّي اتَّهَمْتُ نَصِيْحَ الشَّيْبِ فِي عَذَلِي
وَالشَّيْبُ أَبْعَدُ فِي نُصْحٍ عَنِ التُّهَمِ

Innī-t-tahamtu naṣīḥa'sh-shaybi fī ᶜadhalī
Wa'sh-shaybu abᶜadu fī nuṣ-ḥin ᶜani't-tuhami

12. I even suspected the counsel of my own grey hairs rebuking me,
When I knew the counsel of old age and grey hair to be above suspicion

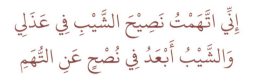

CHAPTER TWO

A Caution about the Whims of the Self

فَإِنَّ أَمَّارَتِي بِالسُّوءِ مَا اتَّعَظَتْ
مِنْ جَهْلِهَا بِنَذِيرِ الشَّيْبِ وَالْهَرَمِ

Fa inna ammāratī bi's-sū'i ma-t-ta^{c}aẓat
Min jahlihā bi nadhīri'sh-shaybi wa'l-harami

13. My foolish reckless self refused to heed the warning
Heralded by the onset of grey hair and old age

وَلَا أَعَدَّتْ مِنَ الْفِعْلِ الْجَمِيلِ قِرَى
ضَيْفٍ أَلَمَّ بِرَأْسِي غَيْرَ مُحْتَشِمِ

Wa lā a^{c}addat mina'l-fi^{c}li'l-jamīli qirā
Ḍayfin alamma bi ra'sī ghayra muḥtashimi

14. And it had not prepared any good deeds to properly welcome
This guest who had turned up on my head unannounced

لَوْ كُنْتُ أَعْلَمُ أَنِّي مَا أُوَقِّرُهُ
كَتَمْتُ سِرًّا بَدَالِي مِنْهُ بِالْكَتَمِ

Law kuntu aʿlamu annī mā uwaqqiruhu
Katamtu sirran badā lī minhu bi'l-katami

15. If I had known that I could not receive him with honour,
I would have hidden my secret from him with dye

مَنْ لِي بِرَدِّ جِمَاحٍ مِنْ غَوَايَتِهَا
كَمَا يُرَدُّ جِمَاحُ الْخَيْلِ بِاللُّجُمِ

Man lī bi raddi jimāḥin min ghawāyatihā
Kamā yuraddu jimāḥu'l-khayli bi'l-lujumi

16. Who can hold back my headstrong soul from the error of its ways,
Just as wild horses are restrained with bridles and reins?

فَلَا تَرُمْ بِالْمَعَاصِي كَسْرَ شَهْوَتِهَا
إِنَّ الطَّعَامَ يُقَوِّي شَهْوَةَ النَّهِمِ

Fa lā tarum bi'l-maʿāṣī kasra shahwatihā
Inna'ṭ-ṭaʿāma yuqawwī shahwata'n-nahimi

17. Do not aim to break the desires by plunging further into sin,
The glutton's greed is only increased by [the sight of] food

وَالنَّفْسُ كَالطِّفْلِ إِنْ تُهْمِلْهُ شَبَّ عَلَى
حُبِّ الرَّضَاعِ وَإِنْ تَفْطِمْهُ يَنْفَطِمِ

Wa'n-nafsu kaṭ-ṭifli in tuhmilhu shabba ᶜalā
Ḥubbi'r-raḍāᶜi wa in tafṭimhu yanfaṭimi

18. The self is like an infant, if you neglect its proper care,
It will grow up still loving to suckle;
But once you wean it, it will be weaned

فَصْرِفْ هَوَاهَا وَحَاذِرْ أَنْ تُوَلِّيَهُ
إِنَّ الْهَوَى مَا تَوَلَّى يُصْمِ أَوْ يَصِمِ

Faṣrif hawāha wa ḥādhir an tuwalliyahu
Inna'l-hawā mā tawallā yuṣmi aw yaṣimi

19. So dismiss its passions, beware of letting them take over,
For when passion gets the upper hand,
It will either kill or bring dishonour

وَرَاعِهَا وَهْيَ فِي الْأَعْمَالِ سَائِمَةٌ
وَإِنْ هِيَ اسْتَحْلَتِ الْمَرْعَى فَلَا تُسِمِ

Wa rāᶜihā wahya fi'l-aᶜmāli sā'imatun
Wa in hiya-staḥlati'l-marᶜā fa lā tusimi

20. Keep a watchful eye on it as it grazes in the field of actions,
And if it finds the pasture too delightful, do not let it graze unchecked

كَمْ حَسَّنَتْ لَذَّةً لِلْمَرْءِ قَاتِلَةً
مِنْ حَيْثُ لَمْ يَدْرِ أَنَّ السُّمَّ فِي الدَّسَمِ

Kam ḥassanat ladhdhatan li'l-mar'i qātilatan
Min ḥaythu lam yadri anna's-summa fi'd-dasami

21. How often a pleasure that is in fact deadly has seemed good,
To one who does not know there may be poison in the fat

وَاخْشَ الدَّسَائِسَ مِنْ جُوعٍ وَمِنْ شِبَعٍ
فَرُبَّ مَخْمَصَةٍ شَرٌّ مِنَ التُّخَمِ

Wakhsha'd-dasā'isa min jūʿin wa min shibaʿin
Fa rubba makhmaṣatin sharrun mina't-tukhami

22. Beware the snares of hunger and satiety,
For an empty stomach may be worse than over-eating

وَاسْتَفْرِغِ الدَّمْعَ مِنْ عَيْنٍ قَدِامْتَلَأَتْ
مِنَ الْمَحَارِمِ وَالْزَمْ حِمْيَةَ النَّدَمِ

Wastafrighi'd-damʿa min ʿaynin qad imtala'at
Mina'l-maḥārimi wa'lzam ḥimyata'n-nadami

23. Dry the tears from eyes that have had their fill of forbidden things,
And henceforth let your only diet be regret

وَخَالِفِ النَّفْسَ وَالشَّيْطَانَ وَاعْصِهِمَا
وَإِنْ هُمَا مَحَضَاكَ النُّصْحَ فَتَّهِمِ

Wa khālifi'n-nafsa wa'sh-shayṭāna waʿṣihimā
Wa in humā maḥaḍāka'n-nuṣḥa fattahimi

24. Oppose the self and shaytan – and defy them,
If they try to offer you advice, treat it with suspicion

وَلَا تُطِعْ مِنْهُمَا خَصْماً وَلَا حَكَماً
فَأَنْتَ تَعْرِفُ كَيْدَ الْخَصْمِ وَالْحَكَمِ

Wa lā tuṭiʿ minhumā khaṣman wa lā ḥakaman
Fa anta taʿrifu kayda'l-khaṣmi wa'l-ḥakami

25. Never obey them, whether they oppose or come to arbitrate,
For you know by now the tricks of both opponents and arbitrators

أَسْتَغْفِرُاللّٰهَ مِنْ قَوْلٍ بِلَا عَمَلٍ
لَقَدْ نَسَبْتُ بِهِ نَسْلاً لِذِي عُقُمِ

Astaghfiru Llāha min qawlin bilā ʿamalin
Laqad nasabtu bihi naslan li dhī ʿuqumi

26. I beg Allah's forgiveness for saying things I do not do,
As though I were ascribing progeny to one who was barren

أَمَرْتُكَ الْخَيْرَ لَكِنْ مَاائْتَمَرْتُ بِهِ
وَمَااسْتَقَمْتُ فَمَا قَوْلِي لَكَ اسْتَقِمِ

Amartuka'l-khayra lākin ma'tamartu bihi
Wa ma staqamtu fa mā qawlī laka staqimi

27. I ordered you to be good, but then didn't heed my own advice,
I was not myself upright, so what of my telling you, 'Be upright!'

وَلَا تَزَوَّدْتُ قَبْلَ الْمَوْتِ نَافِلَةً
وَلَمْ أُصَلِّ سِوَى فَرْضٍ وَلَمْ أَصُمِ

Wa lā tazawwadtu qabla'l-mawti nāfilatan
Wa lam uṣalli siwā farḍin wa lam aṣumi

28. I have not made much provision of voluntary prayer
Before death comes to take me,
Neither have I prayed nor fasted more than was obligatory

CHAPTER THREE

On the Praise of the Prophet ﷺ

ظَلَمْتُ سُنَّةَ مَنْ أَحْيَا الظَّلَامَ إِلَى
أَنِ اشْتَكَتْ قَدَمَاهُ الضُّرَّ مِنْ وَرَمِ

Ẓalamtu sunnata man aḥya'ẓ-ẓalāma ilā
Ani-shtakat qadamāhu'ḍ-ḍurra min warami

29. I have done injustice to the path of the one who prayed at night
Until his feet complained of pain and swelling

وَشَدَّ مِنْ سَغَبٍ أَحْشَاءَهُ وَطَوَى
تَحْتَ الْحِجَارَةِ كَشْحاً مُتْرَفَ الأَدَمِ

Wa shadda min saghabin aḥshā'ahu wa ṭawā
Taḥta'l-ḥijārati kash-ḥan mutrafa'l-adami

30. While he bound up his insides against the extremity of his hunger,
Hiding his delicate skin beneath the stone tied round his waist

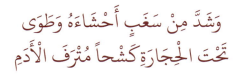

وَرَاوَدَتْهُ الْجِبَالُ الشُّمُّ مِنْ ذَهَبٍ
عَنْ نَفْسِهِ فَأَرَاهَا أَيَّمَا شَمَمِ

Wa rāwadat hu'l-jibālu'sh-shummu min dhahabin
ᶜAn nafsihi fa arāhā ayyamā shamami

31. The high mountains of gold sought to entice him,
But he showed them in return the true meaning of elevation

وَ أَكَّدَتْ زُهْدَهُ فِيهَا ضَرُورَتُهُ
إِنَّ الضَّرُورَةَ لَا تَعْدُو عَلَى الْعِصَمِ

Wa akkadat zuhdahu fīhā ḍarūratuhu
Inna'ḍ-ḍarūrata lā taᶜdū ᶜala'l-ᶜiṣami

32. His situation of austerity and need only confirmed
His indifference to worldly concerns,
For even dire need cannot assail such impeccable virtue

وَكَيْفَ تَدْعُو إِلَى الدُّنْيَا ضَرُورَةُ مَنْ
لَوْلَاهُ لَمْ تُخْرَجِ الدُّنْيَا مِنَ الْعَدَمِ

Wa kayfa tadᶜū ila'd-dunyā ḍarūratu man
Lawlāhu lam tukhraji'd-dunyā mina'l-ᶜadami

33. How could the dire need of such a person draw him towards the world,
When were it not for him, the world would never have emerged
From non-existence?

مُحَمَّدٌ سَيِّدُ الْكَوْنَيْنِ وَالثَّقَلَيْنِ
وَالْفَرِيْقَيْنِ مِنْ عُرْبٍ وَمِنْ عَجَمِ

Muḥammadun sayyidu'l-kawnayni wa'th-thaqalayni
Wa'l-farīqayni min ᶜurbin wa min ᶜajami

34. Muhammad is the master of the two worlds, master of the jinn and men,
And master of the two groups, Arabs and non-Arabs

نَبِيُّنَا الْآمِرُ النَّاهِي فَلَا أَحَدٌ
أَبَرَّ فِي قَوْلِ لَا مِنْهُ وَلَا نَعَمِ

Nabīyyuna'l-āmiru'n-nāhī falā aḥadun
Abarra fī qawli lā minhu wa lā naᶜami

35. Our Prophet, who commands the good and forbids the wrong,
There is no one truer to his word, whether it be 'yes' or 'no'

هُوَ الْحَبِيبُ الَّذِي تُرْجَى شَفَاعَتُهُ
لِكُلِّ هَوْلٍ مِنَ الْأَهْوَالِ مُقْتَحَمِ

Huwa'l-ḥabību'l-ladhī turjā shafāᶜatuhu
Li kulli hawlin mina'l-ahwāli muqtaḥami

36. He is the beloved one, whose intercession is hoped for
Against all the terrifying things that take us by storm

دَعَا إِلَى اللهِ فَالْمُسْتَمْسِكُونَ بِهِ
مُسْتَمْسِكُونَ بِحَبْلٍ غَيْرِ مُنْفَصِمِ

Da^cā ila'Llāhi fa'l-mustamsikūna bihi
Mustamsikūna bi ḥablin ghayri munfaṣimi

37. He has called people to Allah, so those who cling to him
Are clinging to a rope which will never break

فَاقَ النَّبِيِّينَ فِي خَلْقٍ وَفِي خُلُقٍ
وَلَمْ يُدَانُوهُ فِي عِلْمٍ وَلَا كَرَمِ

Fāqa'n-nabīyīna fī khalqin wa fī khuluqin
Wa lam yudānūhu fī ᶜilmin wa lā karami

38. He surpassed the other prophets both in form and noble character,
And none has come close to him in knowledge or in pure generosity

وَكُلُّهُمْ مِنْ رَسُولِ اللهِ مُلْتَمِسٌ
غَرْفاً مِنَ الْبَحْرِ أَوْ رَشْفاً مِنَ الدِّيَمِ

Wa kulluhum min rasūli'Llāhi multamisun
Gharfan mina'l-baḥri aw rashfan mina'd-diyami

39. They all petition the Messenger of Allah for just a handful of water
From his ocean, or a draught from his never-ending rain

وَوَاقِفُونَ لَدَيْهِ عِنْدَ حَدِّهِمِ
مِنْ نُقْطَةِ الْعِلْمِ أَوْمِنْ شَكْلَةِ الْحِكَمِ

Wa wāqifūna ladayhi ᶜinda ḥaddihimi
Min nuqṭati'l-ᶜilmi aw min shaklati'l-ḥikami

40. They all come to a halt before him according to their measure,
As diacritical points upon his knowledge, or vowel marks upon his wisdom

فَهْوَ الَّذِي تَمَّ مَعْنَاهُ وَصُورَتُهُ
ثُمَّ اصْطَفَاهُ حَبِيباً بَارِئُ النَّسَمِ

Fahwa'l-ladhī tamma maᶜnāhu wa ṣūratuhu
Thumma'ṣ-ṭafāhu ḥabīban bāri'u'n-nasami

41. He is the one in whom meaning and form were perfected,
And then the One who created all mankind
Chose him as His beloved

مُنَزَّهٌ عَنْ شَرِيكٍ فِي مَحَاسِنِهِ
فَجَوهَرُ الْحُسْنِ فِيهِ غَيرُ مُنقَسِمِ

Munazzahun ᶜan sharīkin fī maḥāsinihi
Fa jawharu'l-ḥusni fīhi ghayru munqasimi

42. He is far from having any equal in his virtues,
For in him, the essence of perfection is indivisible

دَعْ مَاادَّعَتْهُ النَّصَارَى فِي نَبِيِّهِمِ
وَاحْكُمْ بِمَا شِئْتَ مَدْحًا فِيهِ وَاحْتَكِمِ

Da^c ma-dda^cat hu'n-naṣāra fī nabīyihimi
Waḥkum bimā shi'ta madḥan fīhi waḥtakimi

43. Abandon what the Christians have claimed about their Prophet,
Beyond that you may say whatever you wish in praise of him

وَانْسُبْ إِلَى ذَاتِهِ مَا شِئْتَ مِنْ شَرَفٍ
وَانْسُبْ إِلَى قَدْرِهِ مَا شِئْتَ مِنْ عِظَمِ

Wansub ilā dhātihi mā shi'ta min sharafin
Wansub ilā qadrihi mā shi'ta min ^ciẓami

44. You may ascribe whatever you wish of nobility to his essence,
And to his rank, whatever you wish of greatness

فَإِنَّ فَضْلَ رَسُولِ اللّٰهِ لَيْسَ لَهُ
حَدٌّ فَيُعْرِبَ عَنْهُ نَاطِقٌ بِفَمِ

Fa inna faḍla rasūli'Llāhi laysa lahu
Ḥaddun fa yu^criba ^canhu nāṭiqun bi fami

45. Indeed, the high merit of the Messenger of Allah has no furthest limit
Which could be expressed by the tongue of a human being

لَوْ نَاسَبَتْ قَدْرَهُ آيَاتُهُ عِظَمًا
أَحْيَا اسْمُهُ حِينَ يُدْعَى دَارِسَ الرِّمَمِ

Law nāsabat qadrahu āyātuhu ʿiẓaman
Aḥya-smuhu ḥīna yudʿā dārisa'r-rimami

46. Were his miracles to be as mighty as his rank,
Just the sound of his name would bring dead bones to life

لَمْ يَمْتَحِنَّا بِمَا تَعْيَا الْعُقُولُ بِهِ
حِرْصًا عَلَيْنَا فَلَمْ نَرْتَبْ وَلَمْ نَهِمِ

Lam yamtaḥinnā bimā taʿya'l-ʿuqūlu bihi
Ḥirsan ʿalaynā falam nartab wa lam nahimi

47. He did not test us with things that would exhaust our intellects,
Out of concern for us, so we did not fall into doubt or bewilderment

أَعْيَا الْوَرَى فَهْمُ مَعْنَاهُ فَلَيْسَ يُرَى
فِي الْقُرْبِ وَالْبُعْدِ فِيهِ غَيْرُ مُنْفَحِمِ

Aʿya'l-warā fahmu maʿnāhu falaysa yurā
Fi'l-qurbi wa'l-buʿdi fīhi ghayru munfaḥimi

48. Mankind is unable to comprehend his true essence,
Near and far, they are dumbfounded

كَالشَّمْسِ تَظْهَرُ لِلْعَيْنَيْنِ مِنْ بُعُدٍ
صَغِيرَةً وَتُكِلُّ الطَّرْفَ مِنْ أَمَمِ

Ka'sh-shamsi taẓ-haru li'l-aynayni min buᶜudin
Saghīratan wa tukillu'ṭ-ṭarfa min amami

49. Like the sun, which from afar appears small to the naked eye,
Whereas up close, it would dim and dazzle the vision

وَكَيْفَ يُدْرِكُ فِي الدُّنْيَا حَقِيقَتَهُ
قَوْمٌ نِيَامٌ تَسَلَّوْا عَنْهُ بِالْحُلُمِ

Wa kayfa yudriku fi'd-dunyā ḥaqīqatahu
Qawmun niyāmun tasallaw ᶜanhu bi'l-ḥulumi

50. How can people who are asleep perceive his true reality
In this world, while they are distracted from him by their dreams?

فَمَبْلَغُ الْعِلْمِ فِيهِ أَنَّهُ بَشَرٌ
وَأَنَّهُ خَيْرُ خَلْقِ اللهِ كُلِّهِمِ

Fa mablaghu'l-ᶜilmi fīhi annahu basharun
Wa annahu khayru khalqi'Llāhi kullihimi

51. The extent of the knowledge we have of him is that he is a man,
And that he is the best of all Allah's creation

وَكُلُّ آيٍ أَتَى الرُّسْلُ الْكِرَامُ بِهَا
فَإِنَّمَا اتَّصَلَتْ مِنْ نُورِهِ بِهِمِ

Wa kullu āyin ata'r-ruslu'l-kirāmu bihā
Fa innama-ttaṣalat min nūrihi bihimi

52. Every miracle brought by the Noble Messengers
Was only connected to them through his light

فَإِنَّهُ شَمْسُ فَضْلٍ هُمْ كَوَاكِبُهَا
يُظْهِرْنَ أَنْوَارَهَا لِلنَّاسِ فِي الظُّلَمِ

Fa innahu shamsu faḍlin hum kawākibuhā
Yuẓ-hirna anwārahā li'n-nāsi fi'ẓ-ẓulami

53. Surely he is a sun of bounty and they are its planets,
Manifesting their lights for people in the darkness

أَكْرِمْ بِخَلْقِ نَبِيٍّ زَانَهُ خُلُقٌ
بِالْحُسْنِ مُشْتَمِلٍ بِالْبِشْرِ مُتَّسِمِ

Akrim bi khalqi nabiyyin zānahu khuluqun
Bi'l-ḥusni mushtamilin bi'l-bishri muttasimi

54. How generous the creation of a Prophet
Adorned with excellent character!
So graced with beauty, and radiant of face

كَالزَّهْرِ فِي تَرَفٍ وَالْبَدْرِ فِي شَرَفٍ
وَالْبَحْرِ فِي كَرَمٍ وَالدَّهْرِ فِي هِمَمِ

Ka'z-zahri fī tarafin wa'l-badri fī sharafin
Wa'l-baḥri fī karamin wa'd-dahri fī himami

55. Like a flower in freshness and a full moon in eminence,
Like an ocean in pure generosity and like Time itself
In strength of resolution

كَأَنَّهُ وَهْوَ فَرْدٌ فِي جَلَالَتِهِ
فِي عَسْكَرٍ حِينَ تَلْقَاهُ وَفِي حَشَمِ

Ka annahu wahwa fardun fī jalālatihi
Fī ʿaskarin ḥīna talqāhu wa fī ḥashami

56. Just from his majestic bearing, even when he was alone,
He seemed as if amongst a great army and entourage

كَأَنَّمَا اللُّؤْلُؤُ الْمَكْنُونُ فِي صَدَفٍ
مِنْ مَعْدِنَيْ مَنْطِقٍ مِنْهُ وَ مُبْتَسَمِ

Ka annama'l-lu'lu'u'l-maknūnu fī ṣadafin
Min maʿdinay manṭiqin minhu wa mubtasami

57. It was as if shining pearls, protected in their shells,
Emerged from both his speech and his radiant smile

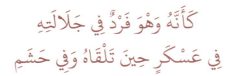

لَا طِيبَ يَعْدِلُ تُرْبًا ضَمَّ أَعْظُمَهُ
طُوبَى لِمُنْتَشِقٍ مِنْهُ وَمُلْتَثِمِ

Lā ṭība yaᶜdilu turban ḍamma aᶜẓumahu
Ṭūbā li muntashiqin minhu wa multathimi

58. No perfume could ever match that of the earth
that holds his noble form,
What bliss for the one who smells that blessed earth or kisses it!

CHAPTER FOUR

On his Birth ﷺ

أَبَانَ مَوْلِدُهُ عَنْ طِيبِ عُنْصُرِهِ
يَا طِيبَ مُبْتَدَإٍ مِنْهُ وَمُخْتَتَمِ

Abāna mawliduhu ᶜan ṭībi ᶜunṣurihi
Yā ṭība mubtada'in minhu wa mukhtatami

59. His birth made clear the purity of his origin,
O how pure his beginning and his end!

يَوْمٌ تَفَرَّسَ فِيهِ الْفُرْسُ أَنَّهُمُ
قَدْ أُنْذِرُوا بِحُلُولِ الْبُؤْسِ وَالنِّقَمِ

Yawmun tafarrasa fīhi'l-fursu annahumu
Qad undhirū bi ḥulūli'l-bu'si wa'l-niqami

60. On that day, the Persians realized they had been warned
Of the onset of misery and disasters

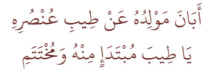

وَ بَاتَ إِيوَانُ كِسْرَى وَهْوَ مُنْصَدِعٌ
كَشَمْلِ أَصْحَابِ كِسْرَى غَيْرَ مُلْتَئِمِ

Wa bāta īwānu Kisrā wahwa munṣadiᶜun
Ka shamli aṣ-ḥābi Kisrā ghayra multa'imi

61. That very night a crack appeared in the Arch of Chosroes[6],
Just as the unity and cohesion of his people was forever lost

وَالنَّارُ خَامِدَةُ الْأَنْفَاسِ مِنْ أَسَفٍ
عَلَيْهِ وَالنَّهْرُ سَاهِي الْعَيْنِ مِنْ سَدَمِ

Wa'n-nāru khāmidatu'l-anfāsi min asafin
ᶜAlayhi wa'n-nahru sāhi'l-ᶜayni min sadami

62. The fire[7], out of grief for the loss, breathed its last,
And the river was distracted from its course by sorrow

وَسَاءَ سَاوَةَ أَنْ غَاضَتْ بُحَيْرَتُهَا
وَرُدَّ وَارِدُهَا بِالْغَيْظِ حِينَ ظَمِي

Wa sā'a sāwata an ghāḍat buḥayratuhā
Wa rudda wāriduhā bi'l-ghayẓi ḥīna ẓamī

63. Sawa[8] was troubled as the waters of its lake receded,
And the one who came to drink from it returned raging with thirst

6 Chosroes - the emperor of the Persians

7 The fire of the Magians, which burned for a thousand years without being extinguished, until the time of the Prophet's birth

8 Sawa - a town in Persia

كَأَنَّ بِالنَّارِ مَا بِالْمَاءِ مِنْ بَلَلٍ
حُزْنًا وَبِالْمَاءِ مَا بِالنَّارِ مِنْ ضَرَمِ

Ka anna bi'n-nāri mā bi'l-mā'i min balalin
Ḥuznan wa bi'l-mā'i mā bi'n-nāri min ḍarami

64. It was as though, from grief, the fire took on water's wetness,
And water took on the blazing dryness of the fire

وَالْجِنُّ تَهْتِفُ وَالْأَنْوَارُ سَاطِعَةٌ
وَالْحَقُّ يَظْهَرُ مِنْ مَعْنًى وَمِنْ كَلِمِ

Wa'l-jinnu tahtifu wa'l-anwāru sāṭiᶜatun
Wa'l-ḥaqqu yaẓ-haru min maᶜnan wa min kalimi

65. The jinn were shrieking, and the lights were flashing out,
As the truth was made manifest in both meaning and word

عَمُوا وَصَمُّوا فَإِعْلَانُ الْبَشَائِرِ لَمْ
يُسْمَعْ وَبَارِقَةُ الْإِنْذَارِ لَمْ تُشَمِ

ᶜAmū wa ṣammū fa iᶜlānu'l-bashā'iri lam
Yusmaᶜ wa bāriqatu'l-indhāri lam tushami

66. But blind and deaf, the Persians did not hear the happy tidings,
Neither did they see the flash of warning signs

مِنْ بَعْدِ مَا أَخْبَرَ الْأَقْوَامَ كَاهِنُهُمْ
بِأَنَّ دِينَهُمُ الْمُعْوَجَّ لَمْ يَقُمِ

Min ba^cdi mā akhbara'l-aqwāma kāhinuhum
Bi anna dīnahumu'l-mu^cwajja lam yaqumi

67. Even after the people's own soothsayers had told them
That their crooked old religion could not last

وَبَعْدَ مَا عَايَنُوا فِي الْأُفْقِ مِنْ شُهُبٍ
مُنْقَضَّةٍ وَفْقَ مَا فِي الْأَرْضِ مِنْ صَنَمِ

Wa ba^cda mā ^cāyanū fi'l-ufqi min shuhubin
Munqaḍḍatin wafqa mā fi'l-arḍi min ṣanami

68. And after they had seen shooting stars away on the horizon,
Falling from the heavens, just as the idols were falling on earth

حَتَّى غَدَا عَنْ طَرِيقِ الْوَحْيِ مُنْهَزِمٌ
مِنَ الشَّيَاطِينِ يَقْفُوا إِثْرَ مُنْهَزِمِ

Ḥattā ghadā ^can ṭarīqi'l-waḥyi munhazimun
Mina'sh-shayāṭīni yaqfū ithra munhazimi

69. Until even the devils were routed, fleeing from the path of revelation,
Following after others as they fled

كَأَنَّهُمْ هَرَبًا أَبْطَالُ أَبْرَهَةٍ
أَوْعَسْكَرٍ بِالْحَصَى مِنْ رَاحَتَيْهِ رُمِي

Ka annahum haraban abṭālu Abrahatin
Aw ʿaskarin bi'l-ḥaṣā min rāḥatayhi rumī

70. They were fleeing just like Abraha's[9] warriors,
Or like the army[10] scattered by pebbles thrown
From the Prophet's own hand

نَبْذًا بِهِ بَعْدَ تَسْبِيحٍ بِبَطْنِهِمَا
نَبْذَ الْمُسَبِّحِ مِنْ أَحْشَاءِ مُلْتَقِمِ

Nabdhan bihi baʿda tasbīḥin bi baṭnihimā
Nabdha'l-musabbiḥi min aḥshā'i multaqimi

71. Thrown by him after glorifying God in the palm of his hand,
As the one who glorified his Lord[11] was thrown out
From the belly of the whale

9 Abraha - a king of Yemen who attacked Makka hoping to destroy the Kaʿba
10 The army of Quraysh during the Battle of Badr
11 The Prophet Yunus, peace be upon him

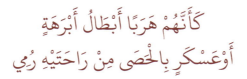

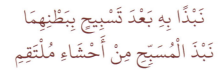

CHAPTER FIVE

On the Miracles that came at his Hand ﷺ

جَاءَتْ لِدَعْوَتِهِ الْأَشْجَارُ سَاجِدَةً
تَمْشِي إِلَيْهِ عَلَى سَاقٍ بِلَا قَدَمِ

Jā'at li daʿwatihi'l-ashjāru sājidatan
Tamshī ilayhi ʿalā sāqin bilā qadami

72. Trees came to him when he called, prostrating,
Walking towards him on trunks that had no feet

كَأَنَّمَا سَطَرَتْ سَطْرًا لِمَا كَتَبَتْ
فُرُوعُهَا مِنْ بَدِيعِ الْخَطِّ بِاللَّقَمِ

Ka anna mā saṭarat saṭran limā katabat
Furūʿuhā min badīʿi'l-khaṭṭi bi'l-laqami

73. As though they had written lines of beautiful calligraphy
With their branches all along the path

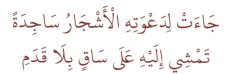

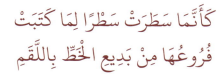

مِثْلَ الْغَمَامَةِ أَنَّى سَارَ سَائِرَةً
تَقِيهِ حَرَّ وَطِيسٍ لِلْهَجِيرِ حَمِي

Mithla'l-ghamāmati annā sāra sā'iratan
Taqīhi ḥarra waṭīsin li'l-hajīri ḥamī

74. Like the cloud that moved with him wherever he went,
Protecting him from the fierce oven of the midday heat

أَقْسَمْتُ بِالْقَمَرِ الْمُنْشَقِّ إِنَّ لَهُ
مِنْ قَلْبِهِ نِسْبَةً مَبْرُورَةَ الْقَسَمِ

Aqsamtu bi'l-qamari'l-munshaqqi inna lahu
Min qalbihi nisbatan mabrūrata'l-qasami

75. I swear by the [Lord of the] moon that was split in two,
Surely it has a connection with his heart,
A true and blessed oath

وَمَا حَوَى الْغَارُ مِنْ خَيْرٍ وَمِنْ كَرَمٍ
وَكُلُّ طَرْفٍ مِنَ الْكُفَّارِ عَنْهُ عَمِي

Wa mā ḥawa'l-ghāru min khayrin wa min karamin
Wa kullu ṭarfin mina'l-kuffāri ᶜanhu ᶜamī

76. And by the excellence and nobility encompassed in the cave[12],
While every glance of the unbelievers was quite blind to it

12 The cave of Thawr outside Makka where the Prophet ﷺ and Abu Bakr ؓ hid during the *hijra* (emigration) to Madina

فَالصِّدْقُ فِي الْغَارِ وَالصِّدِّيقُ لَمْ يَرِمَا
وَهُمْ يَقُولُونَ مَا بِالْغَارِ مِنْ أَرِمِ

Fa'ṣ-ṣidqu fi'l-ghāri wa'ṣ-ṣiddīqu lam yarimā
Wa hum yaqūlūna mā bi'l-ghāri min arimi

77. The true one[13] and the truthful[14] one remained in the cave,
As those outside said to one another, 'There is no one in this cave.'

ظَنُّوا الْحَمَامَ وَظَنُّوا الْعَنْكَبُوتَ عَلَى
خَيْرِ الْبَرِيَّةِ لَمْ تَنْسُجْ وَلَمْ تَحُمِ

Ẓannu'l-ḥamāma wa ẓannu'l-ᶜankabūta ᶜalā
Khayri'l-barīyati lam tansuj wa lam taḥumi

78. They did not suspect that a dove would hover giving protection,
Or that a spider would spin its web to help the Best of Creation

وِقَايَةُ اللهِ أَغْنَتْ عَنْ مُضَاعَفَةٍ
مِنَ الدُّرُوعِ وَعَنْ عَالٍ مِنَ الأُطُمِ

Wiqāyatu'Llāhi aghnat ᶜan muḍāᶜafatin
Mina'd-durūᶜi wa ᶜan ᶜālin mina'l-uṭumi

79. Allah's solicitude and shelter freed him from the need to resort
To coats of armour and fortresses for his protection

13 The true one - referring to the Prophet himself ﷺ
14 The truthful one - referring to Abu Bakr as-Siddīq ؓ

مَا سَامَنِي الدَّهْرُ ضَيْمًا وَاسْتَجَرْتُ بِهِ
إِلَّا وَنِلْتُ جِوَارًا مِنْهُ لَمْ يُضَمِ

Mā sāmani'd-dahru ḍaiman wastajartu bihi
Illā wa niltu jiwāran minhu lam yuḍami

80. Whenever the times have treated me unjustly, and I have turned to him
For refuge, I always found security with him, unharmed

وَلَا الْتَمَسْتُ غِنَى الدَّارَيْنِ مِنْ يَدِهِ
إِلَّا اسْتَلَمْتُ النَّدَى مِنْ خَيْرِ مُسْتَلَمِ

Wa la'l-tamastu ghina'd-dārayni min yadihi
Illa stalamtu'n-nadā min khayri mustalami

81. And never have I sought the wealth of the two worlds from his hand,
Without receiving open-handed generosity from the best of givers

لَا تُنْكِرِ الْوَحْيَ مِنْ رُؤْيَاهُ إِنَّ لَهُ
قَلْبًا إِذَا نَامَتِ الْعَيْنَانِ لَمْ يَنَمِ

Lā tunkiri'l-waḥya min ru'yāhu inna lahu
Qalban idhā nāmati'l-ᶜaynāni lam yanami

82. Do not deny the revelations he received in his dreams,
For surely, though his eyes would sleep, he had a heart that never slept

وَذَاكَ حِينَ بُلُوغٍ مِنْ نُبُوَّتِهِ
فَلَيْسَ يُنْكَرُ فِيهِ حَالُ مُحْتَلِمِ

Wa dhāka ḥīna bulūghin min nubūwwatihi
Fa laysa yunkaru fīhi ḥālu muḥtalimi

83. That was from the time when he attained to prophethood,
For the dreams of the one who has come of age cannot be denied

تَبَارَكَ اللهُ مَا وَحْيٌ بِمُكْتَسَبٍ
وَلَا نَبِيٌّ عَلَى غَيْبٍ بِمُتَّهَمِ

Tabāraka'Llāhu mā waḥyun bi muktasabin
Wa lā nabiyyun ʿalā ghaybin bi muttahami

84. God be praised! Revelation is not something acquired,
Nor is a prophet's knowledge of the unseen to be suspected

كَمْ أَبْرَأَتْ وَصِبًا بِاللَّمْسِ رَاحَتُهُ
وَأَطْلَقَتْ أَرِبًا مِنْ رِبْقَةِ اللَّمَمِ

Kam abra'at waṣiban bi'l-lamsi rāḥatuhu
Wa aṭlaqat ariban min ribqati'l-lamami

85. How many sick people have been healed at the touch of his hand,
And how many, driven almost mad by the noose of their sins,
Have been set free

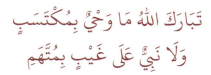

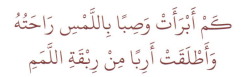

وَأَحْيَتِ السَّنَةَ الشَّهْبَاءَ دَعْوَتُهُ
حَتَّى حَكَتْ غُرَّةً فِي الْأَعْصُرِ الدُّهُمِ

Wa aḥyati's-sanata'sh-shahbā'a daᶜwatuhu
Ḥattā ḥakat ghurratan fi'l-aᶜṣuri'd-duhumi

86. His supplication brought new life in the year of barren dryness,
So that it stood out among the dark years
Like the beautiful white blaze on a horse's forehead

بِعَارِضٍ جَادَ أَوْ خِلْتَ الْبِطَاحَ بِهَا
سَيْبًا مِنَ الْيَمِّ أَوْ سَيْلًا مِنَ الْعَرِمِ

Bi ᶜāriḍin jāda aw khilta'l-biṭāḥa bihā
Sayban mina'l-yammi aw saylan mina'l-ᶜarimi

87. The clouds poured down rain, until you would have thought
The valley was flowing with water from the open sea,
Or from the burst dam of 'Arim

CHAPTER SIX

On the Nobility of the Qur'an and its Praise

دَعْنِي وَوَصْفِيَ آيَاتٍ لَهُ ظَهَرَتْ
ظُهُورَ نَارِ الْقِرَى لَيْلاً عَلَى عَلَمِ

*Da*ᶜ*nī wa waṣfiya āyātin lahu ẓaharat*
Ẓuhūra nāri'l-qirā laylan ᶜ*alā* ᶜ*alami*

88. Allow me to describe to you the signs[15] that appeared to him
Clearly visible like beacons lit at night
On the high hills to welcome guests

فَالدُّرُّ يَزْدَادُ حُسْناً وَهْوَ مُنْتَظِمٌ
وَلَيْسَ يَنْقُصُ قَدْراً غَيْرَ مُنْتَظِمِ

Fa'd-durru yazdādu ḥusnan wahwa muntaẓimun
Wa laysa yanquṣu qadran ghayra muntaẓimi

89. Although a pearl's beauty is increased when strung among others
Its value is not lessened when alone, unstrung

[15] Āyāt - may mean 'signs', 'verses' or 'miracles'

فَمَا تَطَاوُلُ آمَالِ الْمَدِيحِ إِلَى
مَا فِيهِ مِنْ كَرَمِ الْأَخْلَاقِ وَالشِّيَمِ

Fa mā taṭāwulu āmāli'l-madīḥi ilā
Mā fīhi min karami'l-akhlāqi wa'sh-shiyami

90. What hope can the one who tries to praise it have
Of doing justice to its noble traits and qualities?

آيَاتُ حَقٍّ مِنَ الرَّحْمَٰنِ مُحْدَثَةٌ
قَدِيمَةٌ صِفَةُ الْمَوْصُوفِ بِالْقِدَمِ

Āyātu ḥaqqin mina'r-raḥmāni muḥdathatun
Qadīmatun ṣifatu'l-mawṣūfi bi'l-qidami

91. Verses of truth from the Merciful - revealed in time,
Yet Eternal - the attribute of the Pre-eternal One

لَمْ تَقْتَرِنْ بِزَمَانٍ وَهْيَ تُخْبِرُنَا
عَنِ الْمَعَادِ وَعَنْ عَادٍ وَعَنْ إِرَمِ

Lam taqtarin bi zamānin wahya tukhbirunā
ᶜAni'l-maᶜādi wa ᶜan ᶜādin wa ᶜan irami

92. They are not bound by time, and bring us tidings of
The Last Day, and also of 'Ad and Iram

دَامَتْ لَدَيْنَا فَفَاقَتْ كُلَّ مُعْجِزَةٍ
مِنَ النَّبِيِّينَ إِذْ جَاءَتْ وَلَمْ تَدُمِ

Dāmat ladaynā fa fāqat kulla muʿjizatin
Mina'n-nabiyyīna idh jā'at wa lam tadumi

93. They have lasted to our time, and outstripped
Every miracle brought by other prophets,
Which came, but did not last

مُحَكَّمَاتٌ فَمَا يُبْقِينَ مِنْ شُبَهٍ
لِذِي شِقَاقٍ وَمَا يَبْغِينَ مِنْ حَكَمِ

Muḥakkamātun fa mā yubqīna min shubahin
Li dhī shiqāqin wa mā yabghīna min ḥakami

94. Verses so clear that no obscurity can remain
For the wrangler, nor do they require any judge

مَاحُورِبَتْ قَطُّ إِلَّا عَادَ مِنْ حَرَبٍ
أَعْدَى الْأَعَادِى إِلَيْهَا مُلْقِيَ السَّلَمِ

Mā ḥūribat qaṭṭu ilā ʿāda min ḥarabin
Aʿda'l-aʿādī ilayhā mulqiya's-salami

95. No implacable enemy has ever attacked them
Without retreating at last from the battle, begging for peace

رَدَّتْ بَلَاغَتُهَا دَعْوَى مُعَارِضِهَا
رَدَّ الْغَيُورِ يَدَ الْجَانِي عَنِ الْحُرَمِ

Raddat balāghatuhā da^cwā mu^cāriḍihā
Radda'l-ghayūri yada'l-jānī ^cani'l-ḥurami

96. Their very eloquence refutes the claim of one opposing them,
As an honourable man wards off the assailant's hand
From what is sacred

لَهَا مَعَانٍ كَمَوْجِ الْبَحْرِ فِي مَدَدٍ
وَفَوْقَ جَوْهَرِهِ فِي الْحُسْنِ وَالْقِيَمِ

Lahā ma^cānin kamawji'l-baḥri fī madadin
Wa fawqa jawharihi fī'l-ḥusni wa'l-qiyami

97. They contain meanings like the sea's never-ending waves,
And go far beyond its jewels in their beauty and value

فَمَا تُعَدُّ وَلَا تُحْصَى عَجَائِبُهَا
وَلَا تُسَامُ عَلَى الْإِكْثَارِ بِالسَّأَمِ

Fa mā tu^caddu wa lā tuḥṣā ^cajā'ibuhā
Wa lā tusāmu ^cala'l'ikthāri bis-sa'ami

98. Their wonders are numberless and incalculable,
Nor does their constant repetition ever result in weariness or boredom

قَرَّتْ بِهَا عَيْنُ قَارِيهَا فَقُلْتُ لَهُ
لَقَدْ ظَفِرْتَ بِحَبْلِ اللهِ فَاعْتَصِمِ

Qarrat bihā ʿaynu qārīhā fa qultu lahu
Laqad ẓafirta bi ḥabli Llāhi faʿtaṣimi

99. The one who recited them was filled with delight, and I said to him,
'Truly you have seized the rope of Allah – so hold on to it.'

إِنْ تَتْلُهَا خِيفَةً مِنْ حَرِّ نَارِ لَظَى
أَطْفَأْتَ حَرَّ لَظَى مِنْ وِرْدِهَا الشَّبِمِ

In tatluhā khīfatan min ḥarri nāri laẓā
Aṭfa'ta ḥarra laẓā min wirdiha'sh-shabimi

100. If you recite them fearing the heat of the blazing Fire,
You have extinguished the heat of the blaze by their cool sweet water

كَأَنَّهَا الْحَوْضُ تَبْيَضُّ الْوُجُوهُ بِهِ
مِنَ الْعُصَاةِ وَقَدْ جَاؤُوهُ كَالْحُمَمِ

Ka'annaha'l-ḥawḍu tabyaḍḍu'l-wujūhu bihi
Mina'l-ʿuṣāti wa qad jā'ūhu ka'l-ḥumami

101. Like the *Ḥawḍ*[16], which makes bright the faces of the disobedient,
When they had arrived with faces black as coal

16 The Pool of the Prophet ﷺ, where the believers will gather and drink on the Last Day before they enter the Garden

وَكَالصِّرَاطِ وَكَالْمِيزَانِ مَعْدِلَةً
فَالْقِسْطُ مِنْ غَيْرِهَا فِي النَّاسِ لَمْ يَقُمِ

Wa ka'ṣ-ṣirāṭi wa ka'l-mīzāni ma^c^dilatan
Fa'l-qisṭu min ghayrihā fi'n-nāsi lam yaqumi

102. Like the *Sirat*[17], and like the Balance Scales[18] in justice,
True justice among men cannot be established from any other

لَا تَعْجَبَنْ لِحَسُودٍ رَاحَ يُنْكِرُهَا
تَجَاهُلاً وَهْوَ عَيْنُ الْحَاذِقِ الْفَهِمِ

Lā ta^c^jaban li ḥasūdin rāḥa yunkiruhā
Tajāhulan wahwa ^c^aynu'l-ḥādhiqi'l-fahimi

103. Do not be surprised if an envious person refuses to acknowledge them
Affecting ignorance, even though perfectly able to understand

قَدْ تُنْكِرُ الْعَيْنُ ضَوْءَ الشَّمْسِ مِنْ رَمَدٍ
وَيُنْكِرُ الْفَمُ طَعْمَ الْمَاءِ مِنْ سَقَمِ

Qad tunkiru'l-^c^aynu ḍaw'a'sh-shamsi min ramadin
Wa yunkiru'l-famu ṭa^c^ma'l-mā'i min saqami

104. For the eye may reject the sun's light when it is inflamed,
And when the body is unwell,
The mouth may shun even the taste of sweet water.

[17] A bridge stretched over Hell, as sharp as a sword and thinner than a hair, across which all must pass to reach the place of safety

[18] The Balance Scales of the Final Reckoning

CHAPTER SEVEN

On the Prophet's Night Journey and Ascension ﷺ

يَا خَيْرَ مَنْ يَمَّمَ الْعَافُونَ سَاحَتَهُ
سَعْياً وَفَوْقَ مُتُونِ الْأَيْنُقِ الرُّسُمِ

Ya khayra man yammama'l-ᶜāfūna sāḥatahu
Saᶜyan wa fawqa mutūni'l-aynuqi'r-rusumi

105. O best of those to whose courtyards repair the seekers of blessings,
On foot and on the backs of laden camels

وَمَنْ هُوَ الْآيَةُ الْكُبْرَى لِمُعْتَبِرٍ
وَمَنْ هُوَ النِّعْمَةُ الْعُظْمَى لِمُغْتَنِمِ

Wa man huwa'l-āyatu'l-kubrā li muᶜtabirin
Wa man huwa'n-niᶜmatu'l-ᶜuẓmā li mughtanimi

106. O you who are the greatest sign for the one able to perceive,
And the most sublime blessing for the one desiring benefit

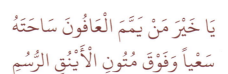

سَرَيْتَ مِنْ حَرَمٍ لَيْلًا إِلَى حَرَمٍ
كَمَا سَرَى الْبَدْرُ فِي دَاجٍ مِنَ الظُّلَمِ

Sarayta min ḥaramin laylan ilā ḥaramin
Kamā sara'l-badru fī dājin mina'ẓ-ẓulami

107. You travelled by night from one sacred place to yet another,
Just as the full moon travels across the pitch-black sky

وَبِتَّ تَرْقَى إِلَى أَنْ نِلْتَ مَنْزِلَةً
مِنْ قَابِ قَوْسَيْنِ لَمْ تُدْرَكْ وَلَمْ تُرَمِ

Wa bitta tarqā ilā an nilta manzilatan
Min qābi qawsayni lam tudrak wa lam turami

108. That night you ascended until you reached a station of nearness
Only two bows-lengths distant,
A station never before attained or even hoped for

وَقَدَّمَتْكَ جَمِيعُ الْأَنْبِيَاءِ بِهَا
وَالرُّسْلِ تَقْدِيمَ مَخْدُومٍ عَلَى خَدَمِ

Wa qaddamatka jamīʿu'l-anbiya'i bihā
Wa'r-rusli taqdīma makhdūmin ʿalā khadami

109. Thus all the Prophets and Messengers gave precedence to you,
The precedence of a master over those who serve him

وَأَنْتَ تَخْتَرِقُ السَّبْعَ الطِّبَاقَ بِهِمْ
فِي مَوْكِبٍ كُنْتَ فِيهِ صَاحِبَ الْعَلَمِ

Wa anta takhtariqu's-sab^c a'ṭ-ṭibāqa bihim
Fī mawkibin kunta fīhi ṣāḥiba'l-^c alami

110. You traversed the Seven Heavens with them,
And you were the standard bearer – leading their procession

حَتَّى إِذَا لَمْ تَدَعْ شَأْواً لِمُسْتَبِقٍ
مِنَ الدُّنُوِّ وَلاَ مَرْقًى لِمُسْتَنِمِ

Ḥattā idhā lam tada^c sha'wan li mustabiqin
Min ad-dunuwwi wa lā marqan li mustanimi

111. Until you left no greater goal for the seeker of eminence and proximity,
Nor any higher station for the one seeking elevation

خَفَضْتَ كُلَّ مَقَامٍ بِالْإِضَافَةِ إِذْ
نُودِيتَ بِالرَّفْعِ مِثْلَ الْمُفْرَدِ الْعَلَمِ

Khafaḍta kulla maqāmin bi'l-iḍāfati idh
Nūdīta bi'r-raf^c i mithla'l-mufradi'l-^c alami

112. All other stations seemed lower in comparison with yours
Since you were proclaimed in the highest terms – the unique one

كَيْمَا تَفُوزَ بِوَصْلٍ أَيِّ مُسْتَتِرٍ
عَنِ الْعُيُونِ وَسِرٍّ أَيِّ مُكْتَتَمِ

Kaymā tafūza bi waṣlin ayyi mustatirin
ᶜAni'l-ᶜuyūni wa sirrin ayyi muktatami

113. So that you would achieve a station of perfect proximity
Hidden from the eyes,
And obtain a secret concealed from all creation

فَحُزْتَ كُلَّ فَخَارٍ غَيْرَ مُشْتَرَكٍ
وَجُزْتَ كُلَّ مَقَامٍ غَيْرَ مُزْدَحَمِ

Fa ḥuzta kulla fakhārin ghayra mushtarakin
Wa juzta kulla maqāmin ghayra muzdaḥami

114. So you attained to every excellence without equal
And you passed alone through every station, far from all others

وَجَلَّ مِقْدَارُ مَا وُلِّيتَ مِنْ رُتَبٍ
وَعَزَّ إِدْرَاكُ مَا أُولِيتَ مِنْ نِعَمِ

Wa jalla miqdāru mā wullīta min rutabin
Wa ᶜazza idrāku mā ūlīta min niᶜami

115. Sublime indeed is the measure of the ranks you have been granted,
Beyond comprehension the blessings bestowed upon you

بُشْرَى لَنَا مَعْشَرَ الْإِسْلَامِ إِنَّ لَنَا
مِنَ الْعِنَايَةِ رُكْنًا غَيْرَ مُنْهَدِمِ

Bushrā lanā maʿshara'l-islāmi inna lanā
Mina'l-ʿināyati ruknan ghayra munhadimi

116. Glad tidings for us, O assembly of Muslims,
For truly we have a pillar of support and solicitude
That can never be destroyed

لَمَّا دَعَا اللّٰهُ دَاعِينَا لِطَاعَتِهِ
بِأَكْرَمِ الرُّسْلِ كُنَّا أَكْرَمَ الْأُمَمِ

Lammā daʿa Llāhu dāʿīnā li ṭāʿatihi
Bi akrami'r-rusli kunnā akrama'l-umami

117. When God named the one who called us to obey Him
The noblest of Messengers,
Henceforward we became the noblest of peoples

CHAPTER EIGHT

On the Martial Struggle of the Prophet ﷺ

رَاعَتْ قُلُوبَ الْعِدَا أَنْبَاءُ بِعْثَتِهِ
كَنَبْأَةٍ أَجْفَلَتْ غُفْلاً مِنَ الْغَنَمِ

Rāʿat qulūba'l-ʿidā anbā'u biʿthatihi
Ka nab'atin ajfalat ghuflan mina'l-ghanami

118. News of his marching out cast fear into the hearts of the enemy,
Just as heedless goats are startled at a sudden noise

مَا زَالَ يَلْقَاهُمُ فِي كُلِّ مُعْتَرَكٍ
حَتَّى حَكَوْا بِالْقَنَا لَحْمًا عَلَى وَضَمِ

Mā zāla yalqāhumu fī kulli muʿtarakin
Ḥattā ḥakaw bi'l-qanā laḥman ʿalā waḍami

119. He continued to meet them on every battle ground,
Until they were cut to pieces by spears,
Like meat upon a butcher's block

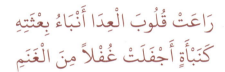

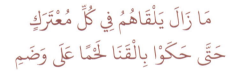

وَدُّوا الْفِرَارَ فَكَادُوا يَغْبِطُونَ بِهِ
أَشْلَاءَ شَالَتْ مَعَ الْعِقْبَانِ وَالرَّخَمِ

Wadu'l-firāra fa kādū yaghbiṭūna bihi
Ashlā'a shālat ma^{c}a'l-^{c}iqbāni wa'r-rakhami

120. They were longing to flee, almost envying
The corpses carried off by the eagles and vultures

تَمْضِي اللَّيَالِي وَلَا يَدْرُونَ عِدَّتَهَا
مَا لَمْ تَكُنْ مِنْ لَيَالِي الْأَشْهُرِ الْحُرُمِ

Tamḍi'l-layālī wa lā yadrūna ^{c}iddatahā
Mā lam takun min layāli'l-ashhuri'l-ḥurumi

121. The nights passed, without them being able to keep count,
Except if they were the nights of the Sacred Months

كَأَنَّمَا الدِّينُ ضَيْفٌ حَلَّ سَاحَتَهُمْ
بِكُلِّ قَرْمٍ إِلَى لَحْمِ الْعِدَا قَرِمِ

Ka annama'd-dīnu ḍayfun ḥalla sāḥatahum
Bi kulli qarmin ilā laḥmi'l-^{c}idā qarimi

122. As if the religion were a guest that had arrived at their courtyards,
With every brave chieftain ready to rend the flesh of their enemies

Chapter Eight – On his Martial Struggle ﷺ

يَجُرُّ بَحْرَ خَمِيسٍ فَوْقَ سَابِحَةٍ
يَرْمِي بِمَوْجٍ مِنَ الْأَبْطَالِ مُلْتَطِمِ

Yajurru baḥra khamīsin fawqa sābiḥatin
Yarmi bi mawjin mina'l-abṭāli multaṭimi

123. Bringing in its wake a sea of armed men upon fast horses,
    Hurling forth waves of brave warriors in clashing tumult

مِنْ كُلِّ مُنْتَدِبٍ لِلَّهِ مُحْتَسِبٍ
يَسْطُو بِمُسْتَأْصِلٍ لِلْكُفْرِ مُصْطَلِمِ

Min kulli muntadibin liLlāhi muḥtasibin
Yasṭū bi musta'ṣilin lil kufri muṣṭalimi

124. Each responding to Allah's summons, seeking His good pleasure,
    Mounting a fierce assault, to tear out unbelief by its roots

حَتَّى غَدَتْ مِلَّةُ الْإِسْلَامِ وَهْيَ بِهِمْ
مِنْ بَعْدِ غُرْبَتِهَا مَوْصُولَةَ الرَّحِمِ

Ḥattā ghadat millatu'l-islāmi wahya bihim
Min baʿdi ghurbatihā mawṣūlata'r-raḥimi

125. Until the religion of Islam, thanks to them,
    After banishment from her homeland
    Was once again united with her kin

مَكْفُولَةً أَبَداً مِنْهُمْ بِخَيْرِ أَبٍ
وَخَيْرِ بَعْلٍ فَلَمْ تَيْتَمْ وَلَمْ تَئِمِ

Makfūlatan abadan minhum bi khayri abin
Wa khayri baᶜlin fa lam taytam wa lam ta'imi

126. Ever protected from her enemies by the best father
And most excellent husband,
So that she was neither orphaned nor widowed

هُمُ الْجِبَالُ فَسَلْ عَنْهُمْ مُصَادِمَهُمْ
مَاذَا رَأَى مِنْهُمُ فِي كُلِّ مُصْطَدَمِ

Humu'l-jibālu fa sal ᶜanhum muṣādimahum
Mādhā ra'ā minhumu fī kulli muṣṭadami

127. They were mountains - ask those who fought against them
Just what they saw of them on every battlefield

وَسَلْ حُنَيْنًا وَسَلْ بَدْرًا وَسَلْ أُحُدًا
فُصُولَ حَتْفٍ لَهُمْ أَدْهَى مِنَ الْوَخَمِ

Wa sal ḥunaynan wa sal badran wa sal uḥudan
Fuṣūla ḥatfin lahum adhā mina'l-wakhami

128. Ask Hunayn, ask Badr, ask Uhud[19] – seasons of death and destruction
More calamitous for them than fatal epidemics

[19] Hunayn, Badr and Uhud were all battles fought by the Muslims against the unbelievers

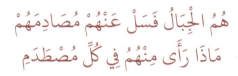

الْمُصْدِرِي الْبِيضِ حُمْرًا بَعْدَ مَا وَرَدَتْ
مِنَ الْعِدَا كُلَّ مُسْوَدٍّ مِنَ اللِّمَمِ

Al-muṣdiri'l-bīḍi ḥumran baᶜda mā waradat
Mina'l-ᶜidā kulla muswaddin mina'l-limami

129. Their burnished swords returned quenched and bloody,
After drinking deep beneath black locks on their enemies' heads

وَالْكَاتِبِينَ بِسُمْرِ الْخَطِّ مَاتَرَكَتْ
أَقْلَامُهُمْ حَرْفَ جِسْمٍ غَيْرَ مُنْعَجِمِ

Wa'l-kātibīna bi sumri'l-khaṭṭi mā tarakat
Aqlāmuhum ḥarfa jismin ghayra munᶜajimi

130. Like writers wielding reed pens for spears,
Their pens left no part of the bodies unpointed or unmarked

شَاكِي السِّلَاحِ لَهُمْ سِيمَا تُمَيِّزُهُمْ
وَالْوَرْدُ يَمْتَازُ بِالسِّيمَا عَنِ السَّلَمِ

Shāki's-silāḥi lahum sīmā tumayyizuhum
Wa'l-wardu yamtāzu bi's-sīmā ᶜani's-salami

131. Bristling with arms, yet a special quality distinguished them,
Just as a rose differs by a certain perfumed quality
From the thorny salam tree

تُهْدِى إِلَيْكَ رِيَاحُ النَّصْرِ نَشْرَهُمُ
فَتَحْسَبُ الزَّهْرَ فِي الْأَكْمَامِ كُلَّ كَمِى

Tuhdī ilayka riyāḥu'n-naṣri nashrahumu
Fa taḥsabu'z-zahra fi'l-akmāmi kulla kamī

132. The winds of victory would present to you their fragrance,
So that you imagine each valiant one of them
To be a beautiful flower in bud

كَأَنَّهُمْ فِي ظُهُورِ الْخَيْلِ نَبْتُ رُباً
مِنْ شِدَّةِ الْحَزْمِ لَا مِنْ شَدَّةِ الْحُزُمِ

Ka annahum fī ẓuhūri'l-khayli nabtu ruban
Min shiddati'l-ḥazmi lā min shaddati'l-ḥuzumi

133. As if, riding their steeds, they were flowers blooming upon a height,
Held there not by the tautness of their saddles,
Rather by the firmness of their resolution

طَارَتْ قُلُوبُ الْعِدَا مِنْ بَأْسِهِمْ فَرَقًا
فَمَا تُفَرِّقُ بَيْنَ الْبَهْمِ وَالْبُهَم

Ṭārat qulūbu'l-ʿidā min ba'sihim faraqan
Fa mā tufarriqu bayna'l-bahmi wa'l-buhami

134. The enemy hearts in turmoil, terrified at their mighty power,
Could hardly tell brave warriors from herds of sheep

وَمَنْ تَكُنْ بِرَسُولِ اللهِ نُصْرَتُهُ
إِنْ تَلْقَهُ الْأُسْدُ فِي آجَامِهَا تَجِمِ

Wa man takun bi rasūli'Llāhi nuṣratuhu
In talqahu'l-usdu fī ājāmihā tajimi

135. Those whose help comes from the Messenger of Allah,
Even lions encountering them in their dens would be speechless with fear

وَلَنْ تَرَى مِنْ وَلِيٍّ غَيْرَ مُنْتَصِرٍ
بِهِ وَلَا مِنْ عَدُوٍّ غَيْرَ مُنْقَصِمِ

Wa lan tarā min waliyyin ghayra muntaṣirin
Bihi wa lā min ʿaduwwin ghayra munqaṣimi

136. You would never see a friend of his unaided by him,
Nor yet an enemy of his undefeated

أَحَلَّ أُمَّتَهُ فِي حِرْزِ مِلَّتِهِ
كَاللَّيْثِ حَلَّ مَعَ الْأَشْبَالِ فِي أَجَمِ

Aḥalla ummatahu fī ḥirzi millatihi
Ka'l-laythi ḥalla maʿa'l-ashbāli fī ajami

137. He established his community within the fortress of his religion,
As the lion settles down with its cubs in its lair

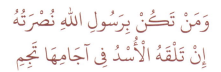

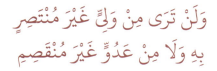

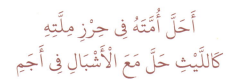

كَمْ جَدَّلَتْ كَلِمَاتُ اللهِ مِنْ جَدِلٍ
فِيهِ وَكَمْ خَصَمَ الْبُرْهَانُ مِنْ خَصِمِ

Kam jaddalat kalimātu'Llāhi min jadilin
Fīhi wa kam khaṣama'l-burhānu min khaṣimi

138. How often have the words of Allah
Thrown down those who contended with him,
How often has the Clear Proof defeated his opponents in argument!

كَفَاكَ بِالْعِلْمِ فِي الْأُمِّيِّ مُعْجِزَةً
فِي الْجَاهِلِيَّةِ وَالتَّأْدِيبِ فِي الْيُتُمِ

Kafāka bi'l-ᶜilmi fi'l-ummiyyi muᶜjizatan
Fi'l-jāhiliyyati wa't-ta'dībi fi'l-yutumi

139. Enough of a miracle for you - such knowledge found
In someone unlettered, living in the Age of Ignorance,
And such refinement in an orphan!

CHAPTER NINE

On Seeking Intercession through the Prophet ﷺ

خَدَمْتُهُ بِمَدِيحٍ أَسْتَقِيلُ بِهِ
ذُنُوبَ عُمْرٍ مَضَى فِي الشِّعْرِ وَالْخِدَمِ

Khadamtuhu bi madīḥin astaqīlu bihi
Dhunūba ʿumrin maḍā fi'sh-shiʿri wa'l-khidami

140. I have served him with my praise, seeking pardon
For the sins of a life spent in poetry and the service of others

إِذْ قَلَّدَانِيَ مَا تُخْشَى عَوَاقِبُهُ
كَأَنَّنِي بِهِمَا هَدْيٌ مِنَ النَّعَمِ

Idh qalladāniya mā tukhshā ʿawāqibuhu
Ka annanī bi himā hadyun mina'n-naʿami

141. Garlanded with these two sins, the consequences of which I dread
It is as though I were now a sacrificial animal

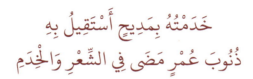

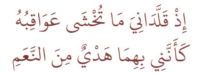

أَطَعْتُ غَيَّ الصِّبَا فِي الْحَالَتَيْنِ وَمَا
حَصَلْتُ إِلَّا عَلَى الْآثَامِ وَالنَّدَمِ

Aṭaᶜtu ghayya'ṣ-ṣibā fi'l-ḥālatayni wa mā
Ḥaṣaltu illa ᶜala'l-āthāmi wa'n-nadami

142. In both these errors I followed only the reckless delinquency of youth
Achieving nothing in the end but wrong action and regret

فَيَا خَسَارَةَ نَفْسٍ فِي تِجَارَتِهَا
لَمْ تَشْتَرِ الدِّينَ بِالدُّنْيَا وَلَمْ تَسُمِ

Fa yā khasārata nafsin fī tijāratiha
Lam tashtari'd-dīna bi'd-dunyā wa lam tasumi

143. Alas for a soul that has met with only loss in its transactions!
It did not use this world to help secure the Next,
Nor even to embark upon negotiations

وَمَنْ يَبِعْ آجِلاً مِنْهُ بِعَاجِلِهِ
يَبِنْ لَهُ الْغَبْنُ فِي بَيْعٍ وَفِي سَلَمِ

Wa man yabiᶜ ājilan minhu bi ᶜājilihi
Yabin lahu'l-ghabnu fī bayᶜin wa fī salami

144. Whoever sells his Hereafter in exchange for this world,
Soon discovers he has been cheated, both in present and future gains

إِنْ آتِ ذَنْبًا فَمَا عَهْدِي بِمُنْتَقِضٍ
مِنَ النَّبِيِّ وَلَا حَبْلِي بِمُنْصَرِمِ

In āti dhanban fa mā ʿahdī bi muntaqiḍin
Mina'n-nabīyi wa lā ḥablī bi munṣarimi

145. If I were to commit a sin, it would not break
My contract with the Prophet,
Nor cut off my connection to him

فَإِنَّ لِي ذِمَّةً مِنْهُ بِتَسْمِيَتِي
مُحَمَّداً وَهْوَ أَوْفَى الْخَلْقِ بِالذِّمَمِ

Fa inna lī dhimmatan minhu bi tasmiyatī
Muḥammadan wahwa awfa'l-khalqi bi'dh-dhimami

146. For I have a covenant of protection from him
By my being named Muhammad, and he is the most faithful
Of all mankind in keeping trusts

إِنْ لَمْ يَكُنْ فِي مَعَادِي آخِذاً بِيَدِي
فَضْلاً وَإِلَّا فَقُلْ يَا زَلَّةَ الْقَدَمِ

In lam yakun fī maʿādī ākhidhan bi yadī
Faḍlan wa illā faqul yā zallata'l-qadami

147. On the Day of Rising, if he does not take me by the hand
Out of pure kindness, then just say, 'What a terrible end!'

حَاشَاهُ أَنْ يَحْرِمَ الرَّاجِي مَكَارِمَهُ
أَوْيَرْجِعَ الْجَارُمِنْهُ غَيْرَ مُحْتَرَمِ

Ḥāshāhu an yaḥrimi'r-rājī makārimahu
Aw yarjiʿa'l-jāru minhu ghayra muḥtarami

148. Far be it from him to ever deprive the hopeful one
Of his generous gifts,
Or to turn back someone seeking refuge
Without treating him honourably

وَمُنْذُ أَلْزَمْتُ أَفْكَارِي مَدَائِحَهُ
وَجَدْتُهُ لِخَلَاصِي خَيْرَ مُلْتَزِمِ

Wa mundhu alzamtu afkārī madā'iḥahu
Wajadtuhu li khalāṣī khayra multazimi

149. For ever since I have devoted all my thoughts to his praise,
I have found him to be the best guarantor of my salvation

وَلَنْ يَفُوتَ الْغِنَى مِنْهُ يَدًا تَرِبَتْ
إِنَّ الْحَيَا يُنْبِتُ الْأَزْهَارَ فِي الْأَكَمِ

Wa lan yafūta'l-ghinā minhu yadan taribat
Inna'l-ḥayā yunbitu'l-azhāra fi'l-akami

150. His bounty will not fail even a hand that is dusty and poor,
For surely the rain may bring forth flowers even on the rockiest of slopes

وَلَمْ أُرِدْ زَهْرَةَ الدُّنْيَا الَّتِي اقْتَطَفَتْ
يَدَا زُهَيْرٍ بِمَا أَثْنَى عَلَى هَرِمِ

Wa lam urid zahrata'd-dunya'l-lati-qtaṭafat
Yadā zuhayrin bimā athnā ʿalā harimi

151. Indeed, I have no more desire for the flowers of this world,
Like those gathered in by the hands of Zuhayr[20]
For his praise of Harim[21]

[20] Zuhayr ibn Abi Salma - a pre-Islamic poet
[21] Harim ibn Sinan - an Arab king famous for his generosity

CHAPTER TEN

On Intimate Conversation and Cherished Hopes

يَا أَكْرَمَ الْخَلْقِ مَالِي مَنْ أَلُوذُ بِهِ
سِوَاكَ عِنْدَ حُلُولِ الْحَادِثِ الْعَمِمِ

Yā akrama'l-khalqi mā lī man alūdhu bihi
Siwāka ᶜinda ḥulūli'l-ḥādithi'l-ᶜamimi

152. O most Noble of all Creation, whose protection can I seek
But yours, when the Great Catastrophe[22] overtakes us?

وَلَنْ يَضِيقَ رَسُولَ اللهِ جَاهُكَ بِي
إِذَا الْكَرِيمُ تَحَلَّى بِاسْمِ مُنْتَقِمِ

Wa lan yaḍīqa rasūla'Llāhi jāhuka bī
Idhā'l-Karīmu taḥallā bismi Muntaqimi

153. O Messenger of Allah, your great rank
Will not be lessened by my petition,
If the Generous One appears as the Avenger

[22] The Day of Judgement

فَإِنَّ مِنْ جُودِكَ الدُّنْيَا وَضَرَّتَهَا
وَمِنْ عُلُومِكَ عِلْمَ اللَّوْحِ وَالْقَلَمِ

Fa inna min jūdika'd-dunyā wa ḍarratahā
Wa min ᶜulūmika ᶜilma'l-lawḥi wa'l-qalami

154. For surely this world and its companion the Next
Are from your generosity. And part of your knowledge
Is knowledge of the Preserved Tablet[23] and of the Pen[24]

يَا نَفْسُ لَا تَقْنَطِي مِنْ زَلَّةٍ عَظُمَتْ
إِنَّ الْكَبَائِرَ فِي الْغُفْرَانِ كَاللَّمَمِ

Yā nafsu lā taqnaṭī min zallatin ᶜaẓumat
Inna'l-kabā'ira fi'l-ghufrāni ka'l-lamami

155. O my soul, do not despair over an error which may appear immense,
For surely even grave sins, with divine forgiveness
Are more like minor lapses

لَعَلَّ رَحْمَةَ رَبِّي حِينَ يَقْسِمُهَا
تَأْتِي عَلَى حَسَبِ الْعِصْيَانِ فِي الْقِسَمِ

Laᶜalla raḥmata rabbī ḥīna yaqsimuhā
Ta'tī ᶜalā ḥasabi'l-ᶜiṣyāni fi'l-qisami

156. It may be that my Lord's mercy, when He distributes it,
Will be apportioned in accordance with the magnitude of sins

23 The Tablet upon which the Divine Decree is inscribed
24 The Divine Pen ordered by God to write all that is to come to pass

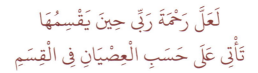

يَا رَبِّ وَاجْعَلْ رَجَائِي غَيْرَ مُنْعَكِسٍ
لَدَيْكَ وَاجْعَلْ حِسَابِي غَيْرَ مُنْخَرِمِ

Yā rabbi waj^{c}al rajā'i ghayra mun^{c}akisin
Ladayka waj^{c}al ḥisābi ghayra munkharimi

157. O my Lord, let not my hopes in You be cast back unfulfilled,
Nor let my firm conviction [of Your Goodness] be thrown into disarray

وَالْطُفْ بِعَبْدِكَ فِي الدَّارَيْنِ إِنَّ لَهُ
صَبْرًا مَتَى تَدْعُهُ الْأَهْوَالُ يَنْهَزِمِ

Walṭuf bi ^{c}abdika fi'd-dārayni inna lahu
Ṣabran matā tad^{c}uhu'l-ahwālu yanhazimi

158. Be kind to Your servant, both in this world and the Next,
For his patience, when called upon by dreadful fears, just disappears

وَأْذَنْ لِسُحْبِ صَلَاةٍ مِنْكَ دَائِمَةٍ
عَلَى النَّبِيِّ بِمُنْهَلٍّ وَمُنْسَجِمِ

Wa'dhan li suḥbi ṣalātin minka dā'imatin
^{c}Ala'n-nabiyyi bi munhallin wa munsajimi

159. And let a cloud of blessings from You pour down
Upon the Prophet, raining down unceasingly

مَا رَنَّحَتْ عَذَبَاتِ الْبَانِ رِيحُ صَبًا
وَأَطْرَبَ الْعِيسَ حَادِى الْعِيسِ بِالنَّغَمِ

Mā rannaḥat ᶜadhabāti'l-bāni rīḥu ṣaban
Wa aṭraba'l-ᶜīsa ḥādi'l-ᶜīsi bi'n-naghami

160. As long as the easterly breezes sway the willow boughs,
And the caravan leader urges on his white camels,
Delighting them with his songs

ثُمَّ الرِّضَا عَنْ أَبِى بَكْرٍ وَعَنْ عُمَرٍ
وَعَنْ عَلِيٍّ وَعَنْ عُثْمَانَ ذِى الْكَرَمِ

Thumma'r-riḍā ᶜan Abī Bakrin wa ᶜan ᶜUmarin
Wa ᶜan ᶜAliyyin wa ᶜan ᶜUthmāna dhi'l-karami

And grant Your good pleasure to Abu Bakr and ᶜUmar
And to ᶜAlī and ᶜUthmān, the noble and generous

وَالآلِ وَالصَّحْبِ ثُمَّ التَّابِعِينَ فَهُمْ
أَهْلُ التُّقَى وَالنَّقَا وَالْحِلْمِ وَالْكَرَمِ

Wa āli wa'ṣ-ṣaḥbi thumma't-tābiᶜīna fa hum
Ahlu't-tuqā wa'n-naqā wa'l-ḥilmi wa'l-karami

And to the Family and the Companions and Followers,
For they are the people of true mindfulness of God
And of purity, forbearance and generosity

يَا رَبِّ بِالْمُصْطَفَى بَلِّغْ مَقَاصِدَنَا
وَاغْفِرْلَنَا مَامَضَى يَا وَاسِعَ الْكَرَمِ

Yā rabbi bi'l-Muṣṭafā balligh maqāṣidanā
Wa'ghfir lanā mā maḍā yā wāsiᶜa'l-karami

O my Lord, by the Chosen One, let us attain all that we are hoping for,
And pardon us for what has passed, O Boundlessly Generous One

وَاغْفِرْ إِلَهِي لِكُلِّ الْمُسْلِمِينَ بِمَا
يَتْلُونَ فِي الْمَسْجِدِ الأَقْصَى وَفِي الْحَرَمِ

Wa'ghfir ilāhī li kulli'l-muslimīna bimā
Yatlūna fi'l-masjidi'l-aqṣā wa fi'l-ḥarami

And, O God, forgive all the Muslims their wrong actions,
By that which they recite in the Masjid al-Aqsa,
As well as in the Ancient Sanctuary[25]

بِجَاهِ مَنْ بَيْتُهُ فِي طَيْبَةٍ حَرَمٌ
وَإِسْمُهُ قَسَمٌ مِنْ أَعْظَمِ الْقَسَمِ

Bi jāhi man baytuhu fī ṭaybatin ḥaramun
Wa ismuhu qasamun min aᶜẓami'l-qasami

By the rank of the one whose dwelling is a sanctuary in Tayba[26]
And whose very name is one of the greatest of oaths

[25] The Kaᶜba and its surrounding mosque in Makka
[26] A name for the city of Madina

وَهَذِهِ بُرْدَةُ الْمُخْتَارِ قَدْ خُتِمَتْ
وَالْحَمْدُ لِلَّهِ فِي بَدْءٍ وَفِي خَتَمِ

Wa hādhihi burdatu'l-mukhtāri qad khutimat
Wa'l-ḥamdu liL!āhi fī bad'in wa fī khatami

This Burda of the Chosen One is now complete,
Praise be to Allah for its beginning and for its end

أَبْيَاتُهَا قَدْ أَتَتْ سِتِّينَ مَعْ مِائَةٍ
فَرِّجْ بِهَا كَرْبَنَا يَا وَاسِعَ الْكَرَمِ

Abyātuhā qad atat sittīna maᶜ mi'atin
Farrij bihā karbanā yā wāsiᶜa'l-karami

Its verses number one hundred and sixty,
Ease, by them, all of our difficulties,
O Boundlessly Generous Lord

The last seven verses were not in the original Burda, but were added at a later date

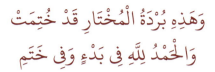

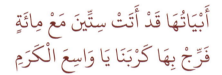

The Mudariyya

THE MUDARIYYA

In Praise of the Best of Creation ﷺ

يَا رَبِّ صَلِّ عَلَى الْمُخْتَارِ مِنْ مُضَرٍ
وَالْأَنْبِيَا وَجَمِيعِ الرُّسْلِ مَا ذُكِرُوا

Yā rabbi ṣalli ᶜala'l-mukhtāri min Muḍarin
Wa'l-anbiyā wa jamiᶜi'r-rusli mā dhukirū

1. O my Lord, pour Your blessings upon the Chosen One of Muḍar
And the Prophets and all of the Messengers whenever they are mentioned

وَصَلِّ رَبِّ عَلَى الهَادِي وَشِيعَتِهِ
وَصَحْبِهِ مَنْ لِطَيِّ الدِّينِ قَدْ نَشَرُوا

Wa ṣalli rabbi ᶜala'l-hādī wa shīᶜatihi
Wa ṣaḥbihi man liṭayyi'd-dīni qad nasharū

2. And pour blessings, O my Lord, upon the Guide and his Followers
And his Companions, those who spread abroad the teachings of the religion

وَجَاهَدُوا مَعَهُ فِي اللهِ وَاجْتَهَدُوا
وَهَاجَرُوا وَلَهُ آوَوْا وَقَدْ نَصَرُوا

Wa jāhadū maʿahu fi'Llāhi wa'jtahadū
Wa hājarū wa lahu āwaw wa qad naṣarū

3. Who fought alongside him in the path of Allah, and struggled valiantly,
Who emigrated, gave him shelter and aided him

وَبَيَّنُوا الْفَرْضَ وَالْمَسْنُونَ وَاعْتَصَبُوا
لِلّٰهِ وَاعْتَصَمُوا بِاللهِ فَانْتَصَرُوا

Wa bayyanu'l-farḍa wa'l-masnūna waʿtaṣabū
LiLlāhi waʿtaṣamū biLlāhi fantaṣarū

4. Who made clear the *farḍ* and the *sunna*, joined forces
For the sake of Allah, clung to Allah and so were victorious

أَزْكَى صَلَاةٍ وَأَنْمَاهَا وَأَشْرَفَهَا
يُعَطِّرُ الْكَوْنَ رَيًّا نَشْرِهَا الْعَطِرُ

Azkā ṣalātin wa anmāhā wa ashrafahā
Yuʿaṭṭiru'l-kawna rayya nashriha'l-ʿaṭiru

5. The most excellent, the most extensive, and the most noble of blessings,
Their fragrant diffusion sweetly permeates the universe

مَعْبُوقَةً بِعَبِيقِ الْمِسْكِ زَاكِيَةً
مِنْ طِيبِهَا أَرَجُ الرِّضْوَانِ يَنْتَشِرُ

Ma^cbūqatan bi ^cabīqi'l-miski zākiyatan
Min ṭībihā araju'r-riḍwāni yantashiru

6. Fragrant with the odour of musk, delightful.
From their scent spreads the sweet perfume
Of acceptance and good pleasure

عَدَّ الْحَصَى وَالثَّرَى وَالرَّمْلِ يَتْبَعُهَا
نَجْمُ السَّمَا وَنَبَاتُ الْأَرْضِ وَالْمَدَرُ

[c]Adda'l-ḥaṣā wa'th-tharā wa'r-ramli yatba[c]uhā
Najmu's-samā wa nabātu'l-arḍi wa'l-madaru

7. In quantity as great as the pebbles, the moist earth, the grains of sand,
Followed by the stars in the heavens,
Plants of the earth and mounds of clay

وَعَدَّ وَزْنِ مَثَاقِيلِ الْجِبَالِ كَمَا
يَلِيهِ قَطْرُ جَمِيعِ الْمَاءِ وَالْمَطَرُ

Wa [c]adda wazni mathāqīli'l-jibāli kamā
Yalīhi qaṭru jamī[c]i'l-mā'i wa'l-maṭaru

8. As great as the measure of the weight of the mountains,
And the drops of all the water and all the rain

وَعَدَّ مَا حَوَتِ الْأَشْجَارُ مِنْ وَرَقٍ
وَكُلِّ حَرْفٍ غَدَا يُتْلَى وَيُسْتَطَرُ

Wa ʿadda mā ḥawati'l-ashjāru min waraqin
Wa kulli ḥarfin ghadā yutlā wa yustaṭaru

9. In number as great as the leaves of all the trees,
And every letter or character that will be read or written

وَالْوَحْشِ وَالطَّيْرِ وَالْأَسْمَاكِ مَعْ نَعَمٍ
يَلِيهِمُ الْجِنُّ وَالْأَمْلَاكُ وَالْبَشَرُ

Wa'l-waḥshi wa'ṭ-ṭayri wa'l-asmāki maʿ naʿamin
Yalīhimu'l-jinnu wa'l-amlāku wa'l-basharu

10. In number as great as the wild animals, the birds, fish and cattle
Followed by the jinn, the angels and human beings

وَالذَّرُّ وَالنَّمْلُ مَعْ جَمْعِ الْحُبُوبِ كَذَا
وَالشَّعْرُ وَالصُّوفُ وَالْأَرْيَاشُ وَالْوَبَرُ

Wa'dh-dharru wa'n-namlu maʿ jamʿi'l-ḥubūbi kadhā
Wa'sh-shaʿru wa'ṣ-ṣūfu wa'l-aryāshu wa'l-wabaru

11. The tiny motes and the ants, all the kernels of grain,
As well as hair and wool, feathers and animal fur

وَمَا أَحَاطَ بِهِ الْعِلْمُ الْمُحِيطُ وَمَا
جَرَى بِهِ الْقَلَمُ الْمَأْمُورُ وَالْقَدَرُ

Wa mā aḥāṭa bihi'l-ᶜilmu'l-muḥīṭu wa mā
Jarā bihi'l-qalamu'l-ma'mūru wa'l-qadaru

12. And all that which comprises the total sum of knowledge,
And whatever was brought by the commanded Pen and the Divine Decree

وَعَدَّ نَعْمَائِكَ اللَّاتِي مَنَنْتَ بِهَا
على الْخَلَائِقِ مُذْ كَانُوا وَمُذْ حُشِرُوا

Wa ᶜadda naᶜmā'ika'llātī mananta bihā
ᶜAla'l-khalā'iqi mudh kānū wa mudh ḥushirū

13. In number as great as Your favours,
Which You have bestowed upon created beings,
Ever since they came into being and were gathered together

وَعَدَّ مِقْدَارِهِ السَّامِي الَّذِي شَرُفَتْ
بِهِ النَّبِيُّونَ وَالْأَمْلَاكُ وَافْتَخَرُوا

Wa ᶜadda miqdārihi's-sāmī lladhī sharufat
Bihi'n-nabiyyūna wa'l-amlāku wa'ftakharū

14. As great as his lofty degree
By which the Prophets and the angels were ennobled,
And they took pride in this

وَعَدَّ مَا كَانَ فِي الأَكْوَانِ يَاسَنَدِي
وَمَا يَكُونُ إِلَى أَنْ تُبْعَثَ الصُّوَرُ

Wa ᶜadda mā kāna fi'l-akwāni yā sanadī
Wa mā yakūnu ilā an tubᶜatha'ṣ-ṣuwaru

15. As great as whatever exists in all the universes, O my Support,
And whatever is still to come into existence,
Until the Day when the forms will be resurrected

فِي كُلِّ طَرْفَةِ عَيْنٍ يَطْرِفُونَ بِهَا
أَهْلُ السَّمَاوَاتِ وَالأَرْضِينَ أَوْ يَذَرُوا

Fī kulli ṭarfati ᶜaynin yaṭrifūna bihā
Ahlu's-samāwāti wa'l-arḍīna aw yadharū

16. In every twinkling of the eye by which
The people of the heavens and the earths
Glance or cease to glance

مِلْءَ السَّمَاوَاتِ وَالأَرْضِينَ مَعْ جَبَلٍ
وَالْفَرْشِ وَالْعَرْشِ وَالْكُرْسِي وَمَا حَصَرُوا

Mil'a's-samāwāti wa'l-arḍīna maᶜ jabalin
Wa'l-farshi wa'l-ᶜarshi wa'l-kursī wa mā ḥaṣarū

17. Whatever fills the heavens and the earths,
Together with the mountains, the spread-out earth,
The Throne, the Footstool and all they contain

مَا أَعْدَمَ اللهُ مَوْجُوداً وَأَوْجَدَ مَعْـ
ـدُوماً صَلَاةً دَوَاماً لَيْسَ تَنْحَصِرُ

Mā aᶜdama Llāhu mawjūdan wa awjada maᶜ
-dūman ṣalātan dawāman laysa tanḥaṣiru

18. Whatever existing thing Allah has caused to vanish,
Or whatever non-existent thing He has brought into being
Blessings without limit and enduring forever

تَسْتَغْرِقُ الْعَدَّ مَعْ جَمْعِ الدُّهُورِ كَمَا
تُحِيطُ بِالْحَدِّ لَا تُبْقِي وَلَا تَذَرُ

Tastaghriqu'l-ᶜadda maᶜ jamᶜi'd-duhūri kamā
Tuḥīṭu bi'l-ḥaddi lā tubqī wa lā tadharu

19. Whose number lasts through all the ages, as
They are boundless, leaving out nothing, encompassing all

لَا غَايَةً وَانْتِهَاءً يَا عَظِيمُ لَهَا
وَلَا لَهَا أَمَدٌ يُقْضَى فَيُعْتَبَرُ

Lā ghāyatan wa'ntihā'an yā ᶜaẓīmu lahā
Wa lā lahā amadun yuqḍā fa yuᶜtabaru

20. They have no final end and no conclusion, O Mighty One,
And no limit decreed, so consider this well

وَعَدَّ أَضْعَافِ مَا قَدْ مَرَّ مِنْ عَدَدٍ
مَعْ ضِعْفِ أَضْعَافِهِ يَا مَنْ لَهُ الْقَدَرُ

Wa ᶜadda aḍᶜāfi mā qad marra min ᶜadadin
Maᶜ ḍiᶜfi aḍᶜāfihi yā man lahu'l-qadaru

21. In number as great as the multiples of all numbers there have been,
Together with multiplying these multiples, O One Who decrees

كَمَا تُحِبُّ وَتَرْضَى سَيِّدِي وَكَمَا
أَمَرْتَنَا أَنْ نُصَلِّي أَنْتَ مُقْتَدِرُ

Kamā tuḥibbu wa tarḍā sayyidi wa kamā
Amartanā an nuṣallī anta muqtadiru

22. Just as You love, O my Master, and in accordance with Your pleasure
And as You have commanded us to send blessings,
You are the Owner of Mighty Power

مَعَ السَّلَامِ كَمَا قَدْ مَرَّ مِنْ عَدَدٍ
رَبِّي وَضَاعِفْهُمَا وَالْفَضْلُ مُنْتَشِرُ

Maᶜa's-salāmi kamā qad marra min ᶜadadin
Rabbi wa ḍāᶜifhumā wa'l-faḍlu muntashiru

23. Together with peace, to the number of what has been mentioned
O my Lord, and multiply them both so that grace may spread far and wide

وَكُلُّ ذَلِكَ مَضْرُوبٌ بِحَقِّكَ فِي
أَنْفَاسِ خَلْقِكَ إِنْ قَلُّوا وَإِنْ كَثُرُوا

Wa kullu dhālika maḍrūbun bi ḥaqqika fī
Anfāsi khalqika in qallū wa in kathurū

24. All of this further multiplied by Your Right in the breaths
Of Your created beings, whether they be few in number or many

يَا رَبِّ وَاغْفِرْ لِقَارِيهَا وَسَامِعِهَا
وَالْمُسْلِمِينَ جَمِيعًا أَيْنَمَا حَضَرُوا

Ya rabbi waghfir li qārīhā wa sāmiᶜihā
Wa'l-muslimīna jamīᶜan aynamā ḥaḍarū

25. O my Lord, forgive the one who recites it,
As well as the one who hears it,
And all of the Muslims, wherever they may be

وَوَالِدِينَا وَأَهْلِينَا وَجِيرَتِنَا
وَكُلُّنَا سَيِّدِي لِلعَفْوِ مُفْتَقِرُ

Wa wālidīnā wa ahlīnā wa jīratinā
Wa kullunā sayyidī lil ᶜafwi muftaqiru

26. And our parents, our families and our neighbours
For all of us, O my Master, are in great need of forgiveness

وَقَدْ أَتَيْتُ ذُنُوبًا لَا عِدَادَ لَهَا
لَكِنَّ عَفْوَكَ لَا يُبْقِي وَلَا يَذَرُ

Wa qad ataytu dhunūban lā ᶜidāda lahā
Lākinna ᶜafwaka lā yubqī wa lā yadharu

27. I have committed many wrong actions - there is no end to them!
But indeed Your pardon leaves nothing - no sin remains

وَالْهَمُّ عَنْ كُلِّ مَا أَبْغِيهِ أَشْغَلَنِي
وَقَدْ أَتَى خَاضِعًا وَالْقَلْبُ مُنْكَسِرُ

Wa'l-hammu ᶜan kulli mā abghīhi ashghalanī
Wa qad atā khāḍiᶜan wa'l-qalbu munkasiru

28. Worry has preoccupied me from all that I hope to attain,
And it came humbly and with a broken heart

أَرْجُوكَ يَا رَبِّ فِي الدَّارَيْنِ تَرْحَمُنَا
بِجَاهِ مَنْ فِي يَدَيْهِ سَبَّحَ الْحَجَرُ

Arjūka yā rabbi fi'd-dārayni tarḥamunā
Bijāhi man fī yadayhi sabbaḥa'l-ḥajaru

29. I beseech You, O my Lord, to show us mercy
In the two worlds, by the rank of the one
In whose hands pebbles glorified God

يَا رَبِّ أَعْظِمْ لَنَا أَجْرًا وَمَغْفِرَةً
فَإِنَّ جُودَكَ بَحْرٌ لَيْسَ يَنْحَصِرُ

Yā rabbi a^cẓim lanā ajran wa maghfiratan
Fa inna jūdaka baḥrun laysa yanḥasiru

30. O my Lord, increase for us both our reward and forgiveness,
For surely Your Generosity is a sea without a shore

وَاقْضِ دُيُونًا لَهَا الْأَخْلَاقُ ضَائِقَةٌ
وَفَرِّجِ الْكَرْبَ عَنَّا أَنْتَ مُقْتَدِرُ

Waqḍi duyūnan laha'l-akhlāqu ḍā'iqatun
Wa farriji'l-karba ᶜannā anta muqtadiru

31. Settle the debts which leave noble character in difficult straits,
And release us from our troubles, O You Who are Powerful

وَكُنْ لَطِيفًا بِنَا فِي كُلِّ نَازِلَةٍ
لُطْفًا جَمِيلًا بِهِ الْأَهْوَالُ تَنْحَسِرُ

Wa kun laṭīfan binā fī kulli nāzilatin
Luṭfan jamīlan bihi'l-ahwālu tanḥasiru

32. Be kind to us whenever calamities befall us,
With a beautiful kindness which causes all distress to disappear

بِالْمُصْطَفَى الْمُجْتَبَى خَيْرِ الْأَنَامِ وَمَنْ
جَلَالَةً نَزَلَتْ فِي مَدْحِهِ السُّوَرُ

Bi'l-Muṣṭafā'l-mujtabā khayri'l-anāmi wa man
Jalālatan nazalat fī madḥihi's-suwaru

33. By Mustafa, the Elected One, the Best of Creation,
In whose praise *surahs* were revealed to honour him

ثُمَّ الصَّلَاةُ عَلَى الْمُخْتَارِ مَا طَلَعَتْ
شَمْسُ النَّهَارِ وَمَا قَدْ شَعْشَعَ الْقَمَرُ

Thumma's-ṣalātu ᶜala'l-mukhtāri mā ṭalaᶜat
Shamsu'n-nahāri wa mā qad shaᶜshaᶜa'l-qamaru

34. And then prayers be upon the Chosen One
As long as the sun shines upon the day,
And the moon casts its radiance about

ثُمَّ الرِّضَا عَنْ أَبِي بَكْرٍ خَلِيفَتِهِ
مَنْ قَامَ مِنْ بَعْدِهِ لِلدِّينِ يَنْتَصِرُ

Thumma'r-riḍā ᶜan Abī Bakrin khalīfatihi
Man qāma min baᶜdihi li'd-dīni yantaṣiru

35. And may You be pleased with Abu Bakr, his caliph,
Who stood up for the religion after he was gone

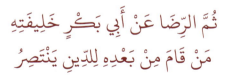

وَعَنْ أَبِي حَفْصٍ الْفَارُوقِ صَاحِبِهِ
مَنْ قَوْلُهُ الْفَصْلُ فِي أَحْكَامِهِ عُمَرُ

Wa ᶜan Abī Ḥafsin l-Fārūqi ṣāḥibihi
Man qawluhu'l-faṣlu fī aḥkāmihi ᶜUmaru

36. And with Abu Hafṣ al-Fārūq, his companion
ᶜUmar, whose word in his rulings was decisive,

وَجُدْ لِعُثْمَانَ ذِي النُّورَيْنِ مَنْ كَمُلَتْ
لَهُ الْمَحَاسِنُ فِي الدَّارَيْنِ وَالظَّفَرُ

Wa jud li ᶜUthmāna dhi'n-nūrayni man kamulat
Lahu'l-maḥāsinu fi'd-dārayni wa'ẓ-ẓafaru

37. And bestow good upon ᶜUthmān, he of the two lights, for whom
The virtues were perfected in the two worlds, and in the final victory

كَذَا عَلِيٌّ مَعَ ابْنَيْهِ وَأُمِّهِمَا
أَهْلُ الْعَبَاءِ كَمَا قَدْ جَاءَنَا الْخَبَرُ

Kadhā ᶜAliyyun maᶜabnayhi wa ummihimā
Ahlu'l-ᶜabā'i kamā qad jā'ana'l-khabaru

38. And likewise ᶜAlī, as well as his two sons and their mother,
The People of the Cloak, as has come down to us in tradition

The Mudariyya

$$\text{كَذَا خَدِيجَتُنَا الْكُبْرَى الَّتِي بَذَلَتْ}$$
$$\text{أَمْوَالَهَا لِرَسُولِ اللهِ يَنْتَصِرُ}$$

*Kadhā Khadījatuna l-Kubra'latī badhalat
Amwālahā li rasūliLlāhi yantaṣiru*

39. And also our lady Khadijah al-Kubra who generously gave her wealth
In order to help and support the Messenger of Allah

$$\text{وَالطَّاهِرَاتُ نِسَاءُ الْمُصْطَفَى وَكَذَا}$$
$$\text{بَنَاتُهُ وَبَنُوهُ كُلَّمَا ذُكِرُوا}$$

*Wa'ṭ-ṭāhirātu nisā'u'l-Muṣṭafā wa kadhā
Banātuhu wa banūhu kullamā dhukirū*

40. And those pure women, the wives of Mustafa,
And his daughters and sons, whenever they are mentioned

$$\text{سَعْدُ سَعِيدُ بْنُ عَوْفٍ طَلْحَةُ وَأَبُو}$$
$$\text{عُبَيْدَةٍ وَزُبَيْرٌ سَادَةٌ غُرَرُ}$$

*Saʿdun, Saʿīdu-bnu ʿAwfin, Ṭalḥatun wa Abū
ʿUbaydatin wa Zubayrun sādatun ghuraru*

41. As well as Saʿd, Saʿīd ibn ʿAwf and Ṭalḥa
And Abu ʿUbayda and Zubayr, the finest of masters

وَحَمْزَةٌ وَكَذَا الْعَبَّاسُ سَيِّدُنَا
وَنَجْلُهُ الْحَبْرُ مَنْ زَالَتْ بِهِ الْغِيَرُ

Wa Ḥamzatun wa kadha'l-ᶜAbbāsu sayyidunā
Wa najluhu'l-ḥabru man zālat bihi'l-ghiyaru

42. And Ḥamza and also ᶜAbbās, our master, and his son,
The learned one through whom difficulties were resolved

وَالْآلُ وَالصَّحْبُ وَالْأَتْبَاعُ قَاطِبَةً
مَا جَنَّ لَيْلُ الدَّيَاجِي أَوْ بَدَا السَّحَرُ

Wa'l-ālu wa'ṣ-ṣaḥbu wa'l-atbāᶜu qāṭibatan
Mā janna laylu'd-dayājī aw bada's-saḥaru

43. And all the Family and Companions, and all the Followers,
As long as darkness still falls upon the night,
And the dawn reappears

مَعَ الرِّضَا مِنْكَ فِي عَفْوٍ وَعَافِيَةٍ
وَحُسْنِ خَاتِمَةٍ إِنْ يَنْقَضِي الْعُمُرُ

Maᶜa'r-riḍā minka fī ᶜafwin wa ᶜāfiyatin
Wa ḥusni khātimatin in yanqaḍi'l-ᶜumuru

44. Bless them with good pleasure from You in pardon and well-being
And with a good ending when life draws to a close.

The Muhammadiyya

THE MUHAMMADIYYA

مُحَمَّدٌ أَشْرَفُ الْأَعْرَابِ وَالْعَجَمِ
مُحَمَّدٌ خَيْرُ مَنْ يَمْشِي عَلَى قَدَمِ

Muḥammadun ashrafu'l-aᶜrābi wa'l-ᶜajami
Muḥammadun khayru man yamshī ᶜalā qadami

1. Muḥammad - noblest of the Arabs and the non-Arabs
Muḥammad - best of all those who walk upon two feet

مُحَمَّدٌ بَاسِطُ الْمَعْرُوفِ جَامِعُهُ
مُحَمَّدٌ صَاحِبُ الْإِحْسَانِ وَالْكَرَمِ

Muḥammadun bāsiṭu'l-maᶜrūfi jāmiᶜuhu
Muḥammadun ṣāhibu'l-iḥsāni wa'l-karami

2. Muḥammad - most expansive giver of all good things
Muḥammad - the master of excellence and generosity

مُحَمَّدٌ تَاجُ رُسْلِ اللهِ قَاطِبَةً
مُحَمَّدٌ صَادِقُ الْأَقْوَالِ وَالْكَلِمِ

Muḥammadun tāju rusli'Llāhi qāṭibatan
Muḥammadun ṣādiqu'l-aqwāli wa'l-kalimi

3. Muḥammad - crown of the Messengers of God without exception
Muḥammad - in speech and word the one most true

مُحَمَّدٌ ثَابِتُ الْمِيثَاقِ حَافِظُهُ
مُحَمَّدٌ طَيِّبُ الْأَخْلَاقِ وَالشِّيَمِ

Muḥammadun thābitu'l-mīthāqi ḥāfiẓuhu
Muḥammadun ṭayyibu'l-akhlāqi wa'sh-shiyami

4. Muḥammad - utterly reliable in keeping trusts
Muḥammad - whose character and qualities are excellent indeed

مُحَمَّدٌ رُوِيَتْ بِالنُّورِ طِينَتُهُ
مُحَمَّدٌ لَمْ يَزَلْ نُورًا مِنَ الْقِدَمِ

Muḥammadun ruwiyat bi'n-nūri ṭīnatuhu
Muḥammadun lam yazal nūran mina'l-qidami

5. Muḥammad - his substance watered by light
Muḥammad - a light still shining from before eternity

مُحَمَّدٌ حَاكِمٌ بِالْعَدْلِ ذُو شَرَفٍ
مُحَمَّدٌ مَعْدِنُ الْإِنْعَامِ وَالْحِكَمِ

Muḥammadun ḥākimun bi'l-ᶜadli dhū sharafin
Muḥammadun maᶜdinu'l-inᶜāmi wa'l-hikami

6. Muḥammad - fair and wise in judgement, the noble one,
Muḥammad - source of kindness and wisdom

مُحَمَّدٌ خَيْرُ خَلْقِ اللهِ مِنْ مُضَرٍ
مُحَمَّدٌ خَيْرُ رُسْلِ اللهِ كُلِّهِمِ

Muḥammadun khayru khalqi'Llāhi min Muḍarin
Muḥammadun khayru rusli'Llāhi kullihimi

7. Muḥammad - finest of God's creation, who came from Muḍar
Muḥammad - of all God's Messengers the best

مُحَمَّدٌ دِينُهُ حَقٌّ نَدِينُ بِهِ
مُحَمَّدٌ مُجْمِلاً حَقًّا عَلَى عَلَمِ

Muḥammadun dīnuhu ḥaqqun nadīnu bihi
Muḥammadun mujmilan ḥaqqan ᶜalā ᶜalami

8. Muḥammad - his creed is true, by it we profess our faith
Muḥammad - eminent, the embodiment of truth

مُحَمَّدٌ ذِكْرُهُ رَوْحٌ لِأَنْفُسِنَا
مُحَمَّدٌ شُكْرُهُ فَرْضٌ عَلَى الْأُمَمِ

Muḥammadun dhikruhu rawḥun li anfusinā
Muḥammadun shukruhu farḍun ᶜala'l-umami

9. Muḥammad - to mention him brings refreshment to our souls
Muḥammad - praising him is a duty upon all peoples

مُحَمَّدٌ زِينَةُ الدُّنْيَا وَبَهْجَتُهَا
مُحَمَّدٌ كَاشِفُ الْغُمَّاتِ وَالظُّلَمِ

Muḥammadun zīnatu'd-dunyā wa bahjatuhā
Muḥammadun kāshifu'l-ghummāti wa'ẓ-ẓulami

10. Muḥammad - the beauty of the world and its splendour
Muḥammad - who lifts the veils of darkness and distress

مُحَمَّدٌ سَيِّدٌ طَابَتْ مَنَاقِبُهُ
مُحَمَّدٌ صَاغَهُ الرَّحْمَـٰنُ بِالنِّعَمِ

Muḥammadun sayyidun ṭābat manāqibuhu
Muḥammadun ṣāghahu'r-raḥmānu bi'n-niᶜami

11. Muḥammad - a master, whose virtues bring delight
Muḥammad - the Most Merciful fashioned him from grace

مُحَمَّدٌ صَفْوَةُ الْبَارِي وَخِيرَتُهُ
مُحَمَّدٌ طَاهِرٌ مِنْ سَائِرِ التُّهَمِ

Muḥammadun ṣafwatu'l-bārī wa khīratuhu
Muḥammadun ṭāhirun min sā'iri't-tuhami

12. Muḥammad - the flower of the Creator and His elect
Muḥammad - pure beyond all suspicion

مُحَمَّدٌ ضَاحِكٌ لِلضَّيْفِ مُكْرِمُهُ
مُحَمَّدٌ جَارُهُ وَاللهِ لَمْ يُضَمِ

Muḥammadun ḍāḥikun li-ḍ-ḍayfi mukrimuhu
Muḥammadun jāruhu wa'Llāhi lam yuḍami

13. Muḥammad - smiling and cheerful with his guest to honour him,
Muḥammad - by God, no neighbour of his was ever wronged!

مُحَمَّدٌ طَابَتِ الدُّنْيَا بِبِعْثَتِهِ
مُحَمَّدٌ جَاءَ بِالْآيَاتِ وَالْحِكَمِ

Muḥammadun ṭābati-d-dunyā bi biʿthatihi
Muḥammadun jā'a bi'l-āyāti wa'l-ḥikami

14. Muḥammad - this world was made delightful by his being sent
Muḥammad - he came with signs and with wisdom

مُحَمَّدٌ يَوْمَ بَعْثِ النَّاسِ شَافِعُنَا
مُحَمَّدٌ نُورُهُ الْهَادِي مِنَ الظُّلَمِ

Muḥammadun yawma baᶜthi-n-nāsi shāfiᶜuna
Muḥammadun nūruhu'l-hādī mina-ẓ-ẓulami

15. Muḥammad - our intercessor on the Day mankind is resurrected
Muḥammad - whose light is the guide out of darkness

مُحَمَّدٌ قَائِمٌ لِلَّهِ ذُو هِمَمٍ
مُحَمَّدٌ خَاتَمٌ لِلرُّسْلِ كُلِّهِمِ

Muḥammadun qā'imun liLlāhi dhū himamin
Muḥammadun khātamun li-r-rusli kullihimi

16. Muḥammad - dedicated to God, he of the highest aspiration
Muḥammad - the Seal of the Messengers, every one of them.